Pizzas and Pancakes

Gary the Lemon Cheesecake

Dear Claire

Thanks for taking care of me during a trying time

ISBN: 9798272528827

Imprint: Independently published

First Edition

Content Warning: *This novel is a work of fiction intended for a mature audience. It contains strong language, scenes of death, depictions of drug distribution. The story also deals with mature themes including trauma, grief, mental health, alcohol abuse and blackmail.* ***Reader discretion is advised.***

"One, remember to look up at the stars and not down at your feet. Two, never give up work. Work gives you meaning and purpose and life is empty without it. Three, if you are lucky enough to find love, remember it is there and don't throw it away." —**Stephen Hawking**

Fair warning, you may get hungry reading this. I know I did writing it. Might order a pizza now, actually. Yeah, why not.
   -**Leslie**

Prologue

Hi there, I'm Gary, the inter-dimensional sentient lemon cheesecake. I'm not going to ruin the plot here, or lose it like Paul, but I am going to give you a brief rundown of the steaks. They're delicious. But with respect to the stakes, well, those are huge.

Let's see. Blast, went through all this in the synopsis didn't I. Right, short version:

Grumpy old git of a security guard finds his mate flat as a pancake, loses the bloody plot, starts interrogating combine harvesters and ordering fifty quids worth of crisps. Meanwhile, the real stakes are higher than the teenagers those drug dealing dingleberries are distributing pizzas to.

If you ain't hooked already, what more do you bloody want? Slice of yours truly? Sod off.

Stay lemony,

Gary the Lemon Cheesecake

Chapter 1 - Sodding Pizza

Gravel crunched beneath my boots, the heat of my thermal socks baking my feet. They were bound to smell later—gives the wife something new to moan about, I suppose.

The torch felt cold in my hand, biting against my palm, as I scanned the warehouse for clues and inconsistencies. Nothing seemed out of place. Pallets full of cans, dozens of them, towering to the top of the warehouse.

They'd be filled with various things throughout the week, most likely. Tuna, pineapples, all that sort of stuff. Just empty, boring metal sat in this sodding warehouse, though.

Back outside, the winter chill bit into my face despite my thermals. Still, I breathed deeply with a smile as I once more gazed up at the stars. Beautiful, cosmic light that made me feel so small, so insignificant, yet so alive.

You had to wonder what was up there. Gods? Aliens? Some kind of inter-dimensional sentient lemon cheesecake?

Probably not that last one. Not sure where that even came from—might be spending too much time at improv club. Or maybe not enough time? Couldn't be sure.

Back at the car now, "Securoguard Services" plastered in bright blue vinyl on the side. Bet I look a right tit driving this thing, but whatever—pays the bills. Mary's not exactly got it covered with her part-time cleaning gig. Well, at least she's working.

That stupid Securoguard logo with the shield cost Mark a grand. One whole thousand pounds for something that probably took his designer one whole bloody minute. Ah well, not my company, not my problem.

Turned the key in the ignition, fired the Ford back up. Off to the next patrol it was, then. Farm just outside of Wisbech—apparently cheaper to hire security than it was to replace the stolen diesel from the harvester's fuel tanks.

Guess it had to happen a lot for them to warrant hiring us out. Makes sense—those bloody little—ah bugger, can't think like that anymore can I. Be inclusive and all that other tripe. Still, they're bloody everywhere round here, pinching things, the scallywags. I should thank them though, really. They keep me in a job.

Getting a bit long in the tooth for all this, though, if I'm being honest with myself. Starting to feel more like a young man's game—at fifty-seven, I can count the weeks until I retire, and so can my knackered old knees.

Mary ain't so lucky. She just turned fifty a week or two ago. Think maybe three, actually—can't remember.

Tyres hummed in my ears as I drove towards the farm. Potholes knocked some sense into me as I pulled up by the front gate. Not sure what they spend the sodding road tax on but it ain't the bloody roads, I can tell you that. If I wanted to ride a roller-coaster I'd buy a bloody ticket to Disneyland.

There was Dick, sat in his car, fast asleep as usual. Probably should report that—but I didn't see the hassle. He'd wake up if someone came, probably. Though my headlights didn't seem to stir him.

"Wakey wakey, sleeping beauty!" I yelled, tapping his car window.

Dick about fell out of his chair, spilling his thermos everywhere. I shouldn't laugh, but if that don't wake him up, not sure what will.

"Paul! Bloody hell! Sorry, mate, I just—"

"Yeah, yeah, doesn't matter. You're up now, and I saw nothing. Just don't make it a habit, sleepyhead."

2

"Thanks, Paul. First time it's happened to me in a long while, mate, I—"

"Yeah, I know. Was me who caught you the first time. Was December twenty-third last year—surprised you could sleep in that winter chill at all, honestly, mate." I interrupted. Didn't need the drama or the theatrics—he was awake, alive, and the site was fine. Professional, me.

"Quiet night then, Paul?"

Sigh. The Q-word again.

"Come on, mate. You've worked security long enough to—"

"Paul, mate, I'm sorry," Dick began, cutting me off. "Forgot you—"

"Never use the bloody Q-word in security, mate!"

Couldn't help but laugh. His grin was infectious—though I s'pose he needed to have a sense of humour, father of five. Maybe him and the wife should buy a bloody telly, or a condom or something.

"I'll see you tomorrow then, Paul?" he asked, pouring himself a fresh cup of tea from his thermos. Not sure why he bothered—still wearing enough of it.

"Yes, mate. Same time. Get yourself an audiobook or something, keep yourself awake, yeah?"

He smiled and nodded. Nice bit of practical, professional advice to help him keep alert. The boredom can be pretty tiring, staring at farm machinery all night. And heaven forbid you need to take a shit, farmhouse often locked up tight.

Back on the road I go, off to my next stop on this mundane merry-go-round. School run, this time—see if Josh caught another teenager with a screwdriver. Way he talks about it, he thinks he deserves a medal, bloody kid. If I got a medal for every petty act of stupidity I stopped out on mobile patrol, I'd need another sodding house to store them all in.

Ah, seemed I needed a quick detour before the school patrol after all. Car yelled at me that the fuel was low. Hungry car looking for some delicious petrol.

The winter chill slapped me round the face once more as I pulled myself out the seat. Bloody knees protesting, as usual. Think I need the black pump? No, green. They keep changing things, for some reason.

I sighed, staring off into the dark as the pump whirred away, tank slowly filling. There were times I wished that magic cheesecake would pop up in the sky, maybe make the night more interesting. Wonder what his name would be? Something fancy, I think. Like Chesterfield or Montgomery. Maybe William?

Shop door beeped at me as I pushed it open, bright lights glaring at me. Packs of fags called out to me, but I didn't listen.

"Evening, sir," the cashier said, in barely understandable English. I approved of him learning, though. Good on him, I guess.

"Pump two, mate. I'll take these too."

Tossed in a pack of crisps. Call it dinner, I s'pose. One tap of the plastic and I was off again, back on the road to Josh and his school. No medal for him though—such a shame.

I pulled into the car park, seeing his Micra sat near the hut. I'll never understand how the fat git even fits in the bloody thing, bless him. Still, he's lost a lot of weight since starting this new diet—maybe I should ask him about it. Maybe not.

"Paul! Hi, mate!" he called out, having spotted me pulling up. At least this one never slept—too many of those horrible energy drinks that tasted like battery acid, no doubt. All the bloody kids his age were mad about the things.

"There he is, the saviour—Josh who caught the bad guy with the screwdriver! So how are we tonight, young man?"

I shouldn't tease him, really. I'll give him a swell head. Still, had to make your own fun in a job like mine.

"Good thanks, Paul. Check it out, I'm down another shirt size!"

He got up and stretched out the baggy space where his lard used to be. Credit where it's due, he's done well to shake off that fat. Best not ask about it, seems personal.

"Well done, young man, you should be proud of yourself. So how'd you do it anyway?"

I was sure I was going to regret that. Here we go again. Bloody mouth running away like a lawnmower. One of those bloody robot ones that drives itself around the lawn that Mary wants. Waste of bloody money.

"Oh! Well, I used ketosis actually! Have you heard of the ketogenic diet?"

Bloody hell was he quacking on about? Oh that sodding diet thing. Don't remember asking about it, but I'm sure he'll explain it anyway. What's he on about then?

"So, you eat fat to beat fat! Isn't that clever, Paul?"

Damn, I missed most of that, but eat fat to beat fat sure does sound stupid. Still... can't argue with his results, can I.

"Sounds good, mate. Well done you, keep at it."

Guess I should go soon, plenty more to—say, who's this? Pair of headlights pulling into the car park caught my eye as they beamed our way. What's this then?

"Oh, err, don't worry, Paul, that's just for me." Josh said.

Kid looked shifty, nervous even. What was he up to here? I saw a man jump out of the car, pulled up next to mine, with a large cardboard box. Oh, tubby's ordered himself a bloody pizza!

Eyebrow raised, grin on my face as I watched Josh take the box. His cheeks cherry red—adorable.

"Now that's a lot of calories, Jo—"

"I'm allowed one cheat meal a week, Paul! Shouldn't you go to your next site or something?" he said, cutting me off like a knife through a pizza.

5

Blimey. Must be hangry, guarding that box like it contained the Crown Jewels.

"Don't I get a slice then, young man?"

"Not in the mood for sharing! Sorry, Paul. See you later then," he said, gesturing for me to leave his hut.

So full of it, like most youths these days. Times like this, I'm glad Mary and I didn't bother. Still, he was losing the weight somehow—couldn't deny him that.

But still, that nagged at me, like an itch I just couldn't scratch. He could have spared a poor old man just one slice, couldn't he? Especially if he's on some kind of diet. Well, never mind, his pizza his choice I s'pose. Best keep moving, then.

But now I'm bloody hungry. Sodding pizza.

Chapter 2 - Wine and Zombies

Right, I'm back on the road and heading to the industrial estate next—might even see a rat or two, if I'm lucky. Alien invasion would go down a treat right now, especially if they brought cheesecake.

Sighed hard, checking the time. Barely gone midnight—had another six hours of this shit before home time, and even then I had to head back to Wisbech to drop off the keys.

Never understand why Mark don't just let me take the bloody car home. I'm not exactly far, living in Leverington—literally takes me five minutes to get to the office.

Does he think I'm going to take the bloody car out for a joyride, or something? I'm fifty-seven! I huffed, pulling into the industrial estate, gripping the wheel tight.

Claire should be on guard tonight, watching the fridge factory. Probably plastered with bloody makeup again—not sure who that was for. Rats maybe? Nice bit of glamour for the adoring rodents?

Could be for herself, I s'pose. I'll never understand how women think—specially not the one I'm married to. Probably fast asleep, in front of the telly, another ten-quid bottle of wine drained by her side. Sometimes feels like I'm funding the assassination of her liver, one bloody bottle at a time.

Pulled up by the gatehouse, Claire with her great big grin as usual. Probably helps seeing me to break up the boredom between her catwalks with the rats. Ratwalks?

"Nice to see you, Paul!" she roared, loud as a bloody lion. She better calm down or my damn tinnitus will start playing up again. Your reward for years of security touring with a heavy metal band, I guess.

"Hey, Claire. So I just saw tubby—need a new nickname for him, lost so much bloody weight. Still wouldn't share a slice of pizza with me though."

"Greedy bastard," she responded curtly. Gotta grin at that. Bloody professional.

"Anything new here tonight then?"

"Yes, actually! Van of chavs pulled up, said they're here to swap out the generator."

Couldn't help but smile. This old bloody chestnut tree.

"Let me guess, unmarked van, and the second you said you'll need to call a supervisor to co—"

"Off they fucked, yeah," she confirmed, cutting me off.

"Typical, I see this plenty out on mobile patrol. Brian actually let them take one, bloody nitwit. Good work, anyway—I'll make sure to let Mark know," I stated.

You do have to respect a professional. Prided myself on that for a long while, now. Doesn't matter how simple the job seems—if it's worth doing, worth doing properly. Something Dad taught me, all them years ago, and it stuck like gorilla glue.

"Heard from the others then?" I asked, making conversation.

"Nah. Darren texted, Brian didn't, and we never even see Jake."

Sigh. Useless tosser, my counterpart. Full of himself, and full of shit—typical mid-twenties.

"Probably off with his wacky-tobaccy again, Claire. I complained to Mark, car stank of it on my last pickup. Not like the boss man gives a shit though, is it?"

It was annoying having to share a car, but it couldn't just sit idle on nights I wasn't scheduled, I s'pose. Still, stupid stoner could at least smoke it somewhere else, couldn't he?

"Mark is too busy counting his pennies to care, Paul."

"Pennies?" I asked, curious.

"Yeah—he ain't raking it in fist over face anymore, since he lost the doors contract. So he says, anyway."

"Ah. Bless him. He'll find something else, always does. Then make this poor old bugger add it to his rounds!"

That one clearly landed, her laugh like a banshee's shriek in my damn ears. Calm yourself down, Claire.

"Anyway, best get back to it. Night, Claire."

"Yep. See ya."

Off I hopped, back into my car, another half hour I'll never get back gone. Ah well, soon be home time.

Fuck! Stupid beeping alarm on my work phone. Alarm callout at the Fensham farm again—finally, a bit of action maybe.

Though if I'm honest with myself, I thought as I put pedal to metal, probably just a tripped fuse or something stupid like that. Still, off I go, focusing on the road ahead, hum of the tyres matching the ringing in my ears.

The headlights of other drivers burned into the back of my skull on the way there. Did they really need to be so bloody bright that they could see into next sodding week?

I pulled up over at the farm, wheel gripped tight. Blaring alarm in my brain already and I haven't even reached the damn panel yet. Boots squelched against the mud as I made my way over to the gate.

There was a sparking at the bottom of the fence, where a dead bat lay. Bloody thing must have flown right into it, got itself fried like a chicken nugget. Do people eat these things?

Still, fence shouldn't have done that. Might be missing something, but the extra crispy bat needed moving. I'll just grab that big stick nearby, give it a prod, reset the box and silence that wailing cacophony. Serve it with chips and ketchup.

Few minutes later, all sorted. Just me, the silence of night and the majesty of those stars. Can't watch them long, though—bloody freezing out here.

Rest of my shift mundane as ever. Same old shit, really. Been decades since I've had any excitement—personally, professionally, in any way that really matters. Times I wondered what the point of me was, really. Zombie apocalypse would spice this up a bit. Maybe that cheesecake I keep forgetting to buy.

I turned my key in the lock, already smelling the stench of red wine lingering in the glass, snores like a lawnmower in my ear. There she was, passed out in her chair again, wine zombie with her bottle drained as usual.

I could wake her. Say something, maybe. Nah. What's the bloody point.

I dragged my aching knees upstairs, went through the motions and got myself in bed. Tomorrow is another day, as they say. Still—I had to admit, I was still a little sore about that pizza. Really wouldn't have killed him to share a slice with me, would it? Was bloody unprofessional, that.

Why am I thinking so hard about this? Just a bloody pizza. Order myself one maybe, bring it to the school and eat it in front of him. That'll make me feel better. Couldn't help but grin at the thought, but I knew it was wicked. Still, time to let it go, and get some sleep.

But it really would be bloody fun, I was sure of that.

Chapter 3 - Zip Zap Boing

My next three shifts were much the same as Monday, really. Same old routes, same old guards, even the alarm callouts were no better. Twenty years doing this—only thing that'd give me pause now is a body or a talking toaster.

Shouldn't wish for such drama, though. Friday night, my night off, and I'm heading to improv club.

Still don't really get what I'm doing here. Just the poster drew me to it, being honest. Sat there on the community notice board of the local corner shop. Improv club, Friday night, seven till late.

Been here a few months now, I think. Not really sure. Still, I'm having fun, even if I'm bloody awful at it.

Community centre stank of stale coffee and the cheapest floor polish money could buy. The usual. Hannah already here, always first to arrive, stacking chairs round the middle. Good to get here on time—last bod in gets suckered with the wonky chair. Probably a health and safety violation, if anyone ever dared inspect the place. I doubt the ghosts even bother anymore.

"Ah! There you are, Paul," Hannah said, gentle smile on her face. Blonde hair down to her shoulders, always arriving early, always setting up before anyone else showed. Professional, her.

"Evening, love," I began, smiling right back. "Need a hand with the chairs?"

"No need, just a couple left. Besides, you know how proud I can be," she mused with a grin.

"Yeah, don't remind me. Still smiling about that sailor skit we did last time. No idea what happened, but Tom was roaring, wasn't he?"

"Sure was! Never seen him so animated. Typical know-it-all detective, cards close to his chest."

"Yeah. Well, I'm pouring a cup of mud before the others show up—want one?" I asked, politely, but hoping she'd say no.

"Not for me."

Good. Couldn't really be arsed making one for myself, much less the both of us.

The others began to trickle in. Stephen, stubble across his chops, up late marking again I can only imagine. Poor git obviously needs another six-week holiday. Bloody teachers.

"Good evening, Gary," I said, nodding at him.

"Stephen, Paul," he grunted back. Miserable sod looked well and truly knackered.

Few more regulars filtered in, including that detective Tom. Same old scowl on his face—made me feel young looking at his expression, and I'm sprinting toward sixty.

"Welcome all! Welcome!" Hannah announced, stood in the centre of the circle. Bright, buzzing fluorescent light above her head only seemed to draw attention to her further, everyone gawping.

"Let's get warmed up. Zip!" she called out, pointing to that guy with the thick glasses.

"Zap," he continued, pointing at me. Bloody hell.

"Zip!"

Ah, bugger it. I knew it was wrong the second I said it. What was that guy's bloody name anyway? Was it Basil? Might have been William.

"Try again, Paul, it's fine," Hannah said gently.

"Boing!" I called out, pointing to Stephen.

16

More zips, zaps and boings and we were finally ready. I mean, I was ready anyway without all the nonsense, but I guess nonsense was kind of the point of tonight, wasn't it.

"Right, let's have some fun. I'll set up the prompt—Paul, let's have you with Stephen to start," Hannah stated.

Right then. Up I get, protesting knees be damned. Let's give this a go.

"Right, Paul, you're going to be a Michelin star chef! Finest in town. Stephen, you're a nervous customer, with a very specific order. Let's go!"

Right then. Chef, I'm a chef. Fancy one, too, with that star thing. I assume the star thing is fancy anyway—honestly haven't heard of it. What do I do? I cook I guess but who? Not bloody who, what! Pancakes?

Stephen pretended to ding a bell to get my attention.

"Hello? Ding ding!" he said.

Bloody hell. Chef, what does a chef do? Cook stuff, obviously. Think, Paul, think!

"Ding ding!"

"Quit your bloody dinging already. Customers these days, honestly. I'm a Michelin tyre chef, mate, you—what?"

Chuckles in the crowd, knocking the wind out of my horse here. What's going on?

"Psst, Paul, it's a star—not a tyre!" Hannah whispered. More titters from the crowd. Bunch of bloody teenagers.

"Ahem! Yes, star chef. Anyway, what you ordering, mate?"

"House special, plea—"

"Out of special, mate. Get you something else?"

"Out? But—"

Stephen looked to Hannah for guidance, as I crossed my arms. Stay out of my kitchen, mate. I'm a star chef. I don't sell tyres.

"Well then, if you're out of special, what do you recommend?"

"Fish and chips, mate."

17

"Don't like fish."

"Chicken and chips then."

"I'm a vegan."

"Chips."

More chuckles from the group. Was I nailing this?

"Paul," Hannah whispered gently, "you have to build on each other. Remember the golden rule—yes, and!"

Yes, and? And what? Oh right, that was exactly the point. Just like she'd been teaching me—build off them, don't shut them out. Right then, let's give this another go.

"Sorry, sir, order something else then?" I said, smiling at Stephen.

"Dragon egg omelette, please," he said, wicked grin on his face.

Dragons? Daft git. Fine, I'll play along then. Why not.

"Right you are, sir. We've got three left—red dragon, blue dragon, or the Welsh one."

Stephen's eyes lit up. "Welsh dragon, please. With a side of—"

"Lemon cheesecake!" I finished. "Obviously. Can't have Welsh dragon without that now, can you?"

"Exactly! Why not, live a little!" Stephen was properly into it now. "And can the dragon egg be... still slightly warm? Like it was just laid?"

"Fresh from the nest this morning, sir. Dragon mother wasn't pleased though. Lost two kitchen staff getting it— but they're both extra crispy if you fancy some mystery meat pie?"

That cracked Tom up. Never seen him laugh so hard. Even Stephen was grinning now, looking a bit less knackered than when he walked in. I thought it was a bit dark myself, even for me. Still, glad to see it land like a plane on a plain.

"Beautiful!" Hannah said, clapping her hands gently. "See? That's the spirit! Now you're playing along."

We sat back down. I was grinning despite myself. Bit ridiculous, the whole bloody thing. But that was the point of it, right?

"Let's have another pair. Tom, fancy it?" Hannah asked.

Tom shook his head. "I'm good watching."

"Suit yourself. Stephen, one more with me?"

Stephen stood again, and Hannah joined him in the circle.

"Right, Stephen, you're a schoolboy who doesn't want to go to school. I'm your mum. Let's see what happens."

Couldn't help but watch Hannah at work. Acting, pretending, playing seemed to come naturally to her. Led the scene without making it obvious, kept Stephen engaged even though he looked like he'd rather be marking essays or on another bloody summer holiday.

Made me wonder why Mary stopped coming after just two sessions. Said she didn't get it, that it wasn't her thing. Fair enough, I s'pose. Not like we did much together anymore anyway.

Could ask her about it. Have an actual conversation, maybe. But not tonight—night's still young, more dragon eggs need cooking, and I'm a Michelin tyre chef.

After the session wrapped up, Hannah caught me by the door.

"You're getting better, Paul. I can see you loosening up a little."

"Loosening up? I'm fifty-seven. Things that loosen up at my age tend to need a doctor."

She laughed. "You know what I mean. You're learning to play. That's what this is all about."

"Yeah, well. Nice to have somewhere to be daft for an hour."

"It's more than that though, isn't it? It's about letting go. Not overthinking, just enjoying the escape."

I nodded, not really sure what to say to that. Too bloody deep for a Friday night.

"See you next week, Paul."

"I'll be here. Night, Hannah."

Walked out to my car—not the Securoguard one, thank Christ, my own knackered Fiat. "Fix it again tomorrow," as they say. Sat there a moment before starting the engine, glad to be rid of the smell of cheap floor polish.

One joy of the week, I'd said. I meant it, too. For an hour on Fridays, I wasn't Paul the security guard, Paul the absent husband, Paul counting weeks until retirement.

I was just Paul. Being daft with dragon eggs and Welsh cheesecakes.

Started the engine. Time to go home to Mary in her chair, wine bottle empty, telly turned to some kind of soap opera. A different kind of zombie apocalypse.

But first—might swing by the chippy. Made myself hungry with that skit, tummy rumbling. Three nights off meant I could afford to eat something that wasn't crisps from a petrol station. I could already smell the vinegar.

Besides, I'd earned it. Dragon egg omelette with cheesecake. Not bad for a grumpy old security guard.

Still wanted a slice of that bloody pizza though. Why was that still nagging at me?

Chapter 4 - Dancing in the moonlight

Weekend passed me by in blissful solitude. For the most part, anyway—Mary sits and watches her soaps, I tend to read in the study. Passes the time.

Been thinking I really should pick up a hobby for retirement. Got my improv club, but that's once a week, and only if Hannah isn't away on holiday. She must make a killing flogging those tractors—doesn't even charge us for the hall hire on Friday nights.

Monday evening here, my security jumper pulled over my head. Bloody shield logo on the back, but at least I don't have to see it.

Off to the office, industrial estate in Wisbech, pick up my motor. I sighed, pulling up to it in my trusty old Fiat. I bet any bloody money I open the door and the stench of cannabis punches me right in the snout, same as last time.

The kid's wasting his damn time. If he smokes that crap, he's going to end up paranoid. Really should bring it up to Mark again—it just isn't professional.

Yep, there it is, I thought as I hacked up half a lung. Sodding weed again. Or herb. Or Mary Jane or... does it really need so many bloody names?

Well, I came armed this time. Hope the young man likes the smell of pine, cos I've got an adorable little yellow tree air freshener to hang over my rear-view mirror. Four nights on, he'll smell nothing but trees. Might end up in a bit of a nose war here, I thought, chuckling away to myself.

You do have to find things to smile about. You don't laugh, you cry, as Mary always said. Well, when we bothered talking to one another, anyway.

Back on the road I went, pine wrestling furiously with the cannabis. Couple of garages, industrial estate, then off to my first guarded site to say hello to Dick.

Wonder if he'll be on kid number six yet. Bloody hell, I'll buy him a telly myself. Maybe a whole box of condoms.

Ah, wait. Darren before Dick on a Monday night, isn't it. Come on, Paul, getting distracted thinking about those cheesecakes again. Right then—off we go.

Here we are, the storage facility. I pulled in, gripping the wheel tight as I parked beside the guard hut. Strange—light's on, but nobody's home. Perhaps he's out on patrol, then. Can't see any torch beams cutting through the night sky, though? Bit odd, that.

Well, no sense sat here musing. I'll try give him a call, make sure he's alright, not tripped and impaled himself on a rusty nail.

Several rings later, voicemail. Twice, in fact. Could've fallen asleep in his car round back maybe? Took a little lunch break, had an accidental snooze. It happens to the best of us, working nights, though it isn't very professional.

I groaned, knees protesting as I left my vehicle. Cold bite of the metal as I gripped my torch tight. Shuffled my way round to the back of the site, to the car park—Darren's car markedly absent, much as he. What's the big idea here?

Try and call him again. Finally, this time I'm through.

"Darren, mate, it's Paul—where are ya?"

"On site, mate, you there now?"

On site? Did someone drop him off, since his car's not here?

"Where? I'm here and don't see you?"

"Just in bogs, mate!"

"But your car isn't here?"

Silence. Something's fishy here, and it ain't the Fillet-O-Fish from that nearby McDonald's. Though looking at that bloody arch is getting me hungry. Still want a slice of that sodding pizza.

"Darren? Where are you? Answer me, mate, I'm worried."

"I'll be there in just a sec—just—just hold on, Paul."

With a click, he ended the call as I made my way slowly back to my car, same old bloody Securoguard logo glaring at me. Sat there a while, waiting, until Darren finally pulled up next to me. The hell is he playing at?

"Darren? What's—"

"Paul, I'm so sorry. Look, just hear me out—I can explain."

Right then. I'm sure this should be interesting. Out with it, Darren.

"Sure thing, mate. I'm listening," I said, waiting for a tall tale. Maybe it was them bloody aliens again.

"I'm not gonna lie to you, Paul—I was moonlighting at the Bear's Paw."

I gripped the wheel of my car tight, knuckles turning white. How bloody unprofessional—he should be ashamed. I sighed deep, shoulders slumping.

"So you locked up here, sodded off to work at that nearby pub, that right?" I asked, perhaps a little curt. Stay professional, Paul.

"Sorry, mate. I don't do this often, I've a kid on the way and—"

"Cut the crap," I interrupted harshly. "You had a good thing going here, double bubble, but it stops tonight. I'm meant to report you for this, Darren."

"Mate, I know. Please, I—"

"Look," I said, interrupting him once more. "I'm not telling the boss about this, but you're going to do overtime if you need the money, not abandoning your post like that. I'm sure a baby on the way is a lot of stress."

Bloody unprofessional. What's he playing at here? Best continue.

"I can't know what you're going through, I don't have a kid of my own, mate. Just never happened for us. But no more abandoning your post here, alright?"

That should sort it. No sense getting Mark involved, would only hurt morale, and I know Darren's a reasonable guy really.

"Paul, mate, thank you. Thank you so much. You're a kind man, caring and—"

"Think nothing of it, just do your job, alright? Job's worth doing, then it's worth doing properly. Dad always told me that. I'll check in with you later."

With that, I fired up the engine. That should sort it, really. End of story. Off I go, back on the road, places to be.

I made the right call there, I'm sure of that. Some professional discretion is good for morale, keep the spirits up. Does get a bit dull being stuck in them little huts twelve hours at a time.

Mark had his way, he'd get me back in static and off the road. Too old to travel all over the shop, he thinks—arrogant prick at times.

Still, good security means good judgement, and I'll give Darren benefit of the doubt on this one. But why's this little incident making me think about that bloody pizza again? Couldn't that bloody kid have just given this old man a slice? Was it really so much to ask?

I gripped the wheel tight, turning sharp as I entered the drive-thru. Just hungry, clearly.

"Welcome to McDonald's, take your order please."

She was chipper for gone midnight on a Monday. Felt myself smiling.

"Yeah, I'll have a cheeseburger please, love."

"Next window."

Pulled up to the window, patiently waiting for her to open it. Wonder what was up there in those cupboards above the fryers? I've never once seen them open one. Think they're hiding all the good stuff in there? Maybe it's the secret ingredient. Assuming they—

"Sir? Cash or card please?"

Tapped my card against the plastic, then fumbled it back into my wallet.

"No worries. Have a good night."

Nice and quick, burger now warming my lap. Wanted the fish, honestly, but they take bloody forever to cook those. Still, dinner was dinner. Wonder what Mary ate tonight? Probably got her calories from a bottle of red. I should look that up, see how many are in a bottle. Curious now. What about pizza? Whole one must be a lot. Must be. How about one slice?

Nothing eventful for the next hour or so, now pulling up to the farm again. Nice to see Dick awake this time, bless him.

"Hey, Paul. I just made a cup of tea—kettle still warm if you fancy one?"

"Oh! Don't mind if I do, mate."

How kind of him. Nice bit of caffeine to keep you going through the night.

"Took your advice, Paul! Got a podcast on my earpiece now. I'm listening to these—"

"Glad to hear." I said, cutting him off tall. Didn't need the life story—just glad he'd found something to keep him awake.

"Well anyway, how are you then? Qu—good night?"

Had to chuckle. That bloody Q-word, seeping through the cracks where it could.

"Yeah. Weekend evaporated, to be honest. Friday was fun, though," I found myself saying as I held the cup of tea he made me. Oh dear—did I get a bit personal myself there? Or had I seen him at improv already? Don't think so. Basil looked a bit like him, though.

"What's Friday then, mate?"

Damn. Piqued his curiosity now, haven't I. Ah well, what's the harm in telling him—he's always been polite to me. Good lad, really, even if he is a bloody narcoleptic.

"Improv club. You get to act daft, really, that's all. Acting, sort of."

I didn't expect his face to light up like a Christmas tree. I seemed to have sparked an interest in him, that Cheshire cat grin anything to go by. No, ginger tabby cat, actually.

"That sounds fun, Paul! How does that work then? Can my kids go?"

Best nip that in the bud before I get distracted thinking about cats again.

"No kids. Not sure I got the time to—"

"Oh come on, Paul. Just a minute? I'm lonely and bored out here, staring at tractors and harvesters all night."

Christ. Unprofessional, but what the hell. Live a little. Besides, it'll just take a minute.

"So it's just about being daft and silly really. We have these prompts, and we pretend."

Don't think I explained that very well, studying his expression. Maybe I'll just show him.

"Right. I'm your dad, you're my ten-year-old son and you don't want to go to school. You get it, Dick?"

"I don't get anything, Dad! What's the point of this school? I'll just end up serving chips at McDonald's anyways!"

"Not if you don't study hard, you won't, son," I said, smiling.

"Wait, what do you mean?"

"Gotta get your degree in McNology, son, or you'll never serve a Big Mac."

Dick burst out laughing—I couldn't help but join in, feeling my chest heave.

"Paul, mate, that is kinda fun. Wacky though, ain't it?"

"Yeah, it's daft. But think that's kind of the point. Like those dragon egg omelettes."

"Uh, what?" he asked, eyebrow raised.

Oh, course. Weren't there, was he. "Sorry, mate, guess you had to be there. You're not Basil."

"When is this club then? Is anyone welcome? Who's Basil?"

Isn't that a bloody herb? Making me hungry now. Bet it goes great on pizza.

"Friday eve, mate, function room at Community centre—just down the road from the Bear's Paw."

"Yeah, alright Paul. I'll come watch you. Not sure if I'm cut out for it myself, though."

"Great, then you'll fit right in. Anyway, mate, back to my rounds. Thanks for the tea," I said, handing him back the mug, settling back into my car. Off I went, more stops to make, before I'm back home to my gorgeous drunk wife.

"Paul, mate, before you go," Dick began.

Bloody hell, what's this all about now then?

"I saw Jake last night, he stopped by. He rarely bothers, but still, I just—"

"Sorry, mate, short on—"

"No, wait, listen, Paul," he said, cutting me off before I had a chance to interrupt. I shut my mouth, studied his face—looked focused, serious somehow. Gotta go, though.

"Look, not sure if I should mention this, but..." he began, scratching behind his ear. "So... Jake had a pizza with him. Asked him for a slice, and he gave it me. But Paul, he had a bunch of baggies stuck to the lid of it, mate. Looked like weed."

I sighed, gripping the wheel tight. "Yeah, I know. Kid's obviously a stoner—car stinks of it every pickup on Monday. But I got an air freshener, so—"

"No, mate," he said, cutting me off once more. Getting annoying, that, bit unprofessional.

"Must have been ten, easy. He ain't smoking all that in a night."

I laughed out loud. "You been watching too much telly, Dick. Just a young, dumb stoner, nothing more exciting than that." I paused a moment, tapping my wheel a little before continuing. "Look, maybe I'll talk to Mark about it end of the week, yeah? I'm off now. Stay awake, mate."

"But Paul, I—"

Off I drove, waving to him. Didn't have the time for crackpot theories—I had a job to do, rounds to make. Easy for him to chat all night, he's only watching one site—I've dozens to deal with. Hopefully without the bloody fried bat this time.

Well, back on the road, tyres humming. Few more stops to do, then it's home to that wine zombie I love so much. For some reason, anyway.

Chapter 5 - Dick Pancake

Rest of Monday was pretty simple. No alarm callouts, no more zapped bat corpses to deal with. Got home to find Mary passed out in the chair again—but she broke out the white wine for once. Must have been a special episode on telly.

Tuesday night, I'm back at the office, picking up my motor again. Ah, that's more like it—fresh scent of pine lingering in my nose instead of that wacky tobaccy. Bloody stoner.

Well, off I go. Stops to make—after more fuel, car dinging away at me, thirsty bugger.

Got my crisps again, packet chucked onto the passenger seat, ready for my break later. Quite a big bag, actually—might share some with Dick when I stop by.

Couldn't help but think back to that little impromptu improv scene between us, as I gripped the wheel tight, focusing hard on the road ahead. It was unprofessional, really, but where's the harm? Just a little bit of fun.

Several hours passed me by, soon time to head to the farm. Josh probably ordering his pizza at the school by now, greedy bastard. I should have crashed that little party instead, told him to respect his elders and give me a slice this time. Still, Dick's on the way first, so quick drop-in at the farm then maybe it's time for school.

All looked fine, looking around as I pulled in. Dick not in the hut, though. Least he isn't bloody sleeping again.

I sat there a while, engine running, heater fighting back the bitter chill of night. Crunched through my crisps waiting for him to get back—I ate the lot, hand to mouth, without bloody thinking about it. Greedy bugger. Won't be sharing them with you after all, Dick. Sorry mate.

Still, though, where is he? Patrol shouldn't have taken him this long—I'd be back myself by now, even with my blasted knees.

Voicemail. Twice, even. Right, best go look for him—he's definitely here, that's his car right there. Still a mug of cold tea in the guard hut, too.

Off I plodded, one foot after the other, squelching in the bloody mud. Tried my best to stick to gravel, but farm after all. Besides, I—Jesus CHRIST!

WHAT THE FUCK!

"Dick!" I called out, rushing over. Not sure why—flat as a fucking pancake. Squished under a fucking harvester—looks like it fell off the front of the... tractory bit.

I felt myself breathing fast. Fast as if I'd been sprinting, running miles. Put my hand against the wall nearby, closing my eyes just a moment. Opened them again. Dick, pancake. Dick pancake.

Deep breath in. One, two, ten. Deep breath out. Action.

"Emergen—"

"Ambulance." I cut her off, hands shaking. Dick's lifeless, gormless face staring up into the sky, the rest of him pancaked.

"Norfolk Amb—"

I cut her off too, rattling off the three words from the app. Just like Mark taught us—three words and the emergency services knew exactly where you are.

My legs were jelly as I shuffled back to the car. Stay on the line, they said, but I hung up and called Mark. Took him a while to pick up, but to be fair it was gone midnight.

"Paul? What are—"

"Dead. Dick's dead. Dead as a pancake. Dead, Mark. Dick, pancake."

Stay cool, Paul. Stay professional. Breathe in, out. In—

"Bloody hell. Sorry to hear that, Paul."

Sorry to hear that? Sorry to fucking hear that, you stupid arrogant fuck? Man's a fucking tube of toothpaste under a harvester and you're sorry to hear that?

"Yeah. I called emergency," I replied, voice cracking, hands shaking heavily by now.

"Don't touch anything, Paul. It needs to—I mean, you need to look out for yourself at the minute. And you can't interfere, police will do an inquiry. Go home—I'll get Jake in to cover you. Do it myself, if need be."

Breathe in, ten, out. Sorry to fucking hear that. Prick.

"OK, Mark. Not gonna argue. I'll shuffle off soon as I give my statement."

"Sound. Take a few days off, Paul. Jake will take the overtime, I'm sure. Night."

With a click, that call was done. Blues flashing as they closed the distance. Next hour went by in a flash of blue lights and hi-vis uniforms. Ringing in my ears louder than it had been in quite some time.

I was finally home, focusing hard on the drive back, hand gripping the wheel tight as if hanging on for dear life. Couldn't stop bloody shaking no matter how hard I fried.

Fuck. "I'll come Friday," Dick had said, his dopey laugh tolling a bell through my ringing ears. Now he'd never laugh again. And... and all those bloody kids. Fuck.

I sat at the wheel, pulled up in my driveway for what seemed like an eternity. Dick's smile, his laugh, then his feckless, lifeless gaze fighting my thoughts for centre row. Close my eyes, Dick pancake. Open my eyes, same again. He was everywhere and nowhere. Everyone and nothing. Pancake.

31

Can't sit out here in the cold all night though. Be professional, man up, straighten your bloody shoulders. Time to go inside. Chin up, carry on.

"Paul?" Mary asked, rushing up from her chair. She was up late, and only seemed halfway through her wine.

"Yeah. Home early. I—"

I began to shake, her face painted with worry as she stared at me. Not the apathy I'd come to expect—Christ, get it together, Paul.

"What happened?" she asked, sounding concerned.

"Dead. Guard dead. Crushed by a... harvester. I found him. Pancake."

My eyes betrayed me, tears rolling down my cheeks. I wiped them away hastily, but it was no use—more just took their place, like a swarm of unwanted invaders, one after another.

Mary shuffled over, little tipsy looked like. But I didn't care—she hugged me close, long, tight. Her warmth against mine, I held her back, for a moment.

Not bloody professional this, though. Stood here in my uniform, crying away like a kid over spilt blood.

"Sorry, Paul," she said finally, pulling back. "Twenty years since last one."

"Twenty-two," I corrected, memory of James with a hole the size of a basketball blown out of his chest burned into my permanent memory, and quickly wrestling with Dick for space under my eyes. Shotgun to his chest over ten grand. Pitiful—and I found that poor bastard too.

"Go rest, Paul," Mary said flatly, before shuffling back to her chair.

Moment well and truly over, I figured I'd do just that. That is, if Dick's lifeless face, hiding behind my eyelids, will let me. I'm in for a long bloody night, I'm sure. Pizzas and pancakes.

Chapter 6 - Flat as a pancake

Dick and James, competing with one another for time beneath my eyelids throughout the night. Sleep? What's that then?

No sense laying here all sodding day. Got myself up, dressed, and a cup of mud. Mary's already off—think she's cleaning the school today. Maybe the office, can't remember.

All I seem to remember is Dick pancake at the minute. Poor bloody bastard. Felt the warm coffee mug against my hands, watching steam linger in the air. Hope his family will be alright. Can imagine they're having a worse day than I am. Christ, Dick, all those bloody kids you left behind.

And all because you stepped under a harvester at the wrong moment. I'm sure we'll get some kind of "safety procedures exist for a reason" email from the bossman sooner or later.

Sorry to hear that. Those four words kept buzzing in my brain, gnawing away at me. What a thing to say, really. How about, you know, holy shit, what happened? Or fuck, you're kidding? Or just something. Not some practised, don't-give-a-shit "sorry to hear that" from some feckless manager earning twice what I do for not even doing my job.

You'd think he dealt with a body every week, how bloody cold he was. We really are just numbers to him, I s'pose. Shame that—never thought he was a bad boss or a bad bloke, but last night got under my skin. Sorry to hear that.

I sighed, finishing the last of my coffee as the bitter taste shocked my tongue. Maybe I'm just tired and cranky? We all process things differently, I s'pose, and it ain't like Mark is the poor bastard that found the Dick pancake now, is it.

Still, I can't just sit about here all day. I think I'm going to go down to the corner shop, find Mary some chocolates. I stared at my empty coffee mug, frowning, thinking back to her arms around me last night. Love's still there, I'm sure, but still feels like an ocean between us.

Bitter chill of winter morning hit me like a shovel round the face. Or a harvester to the pancake, maybe. I walked a little faster, knees be damned, reaching the corner shop.

"Morning, Mr Paul," the heavily accented Indian chap said. Like this guy, always open, learns your name, genuinely gives a shit. Rare attitude to have these days.

"Morning, Jayir. Hope you're well."

"Yes, sir, I am always. Is good to see you."

He's sweet really, I thought, nodding and smiling at him. I grabbed the chocolates Mary likes, those weird bloody shell things that taste like plastic. Whatever—not my treat, hers, isn't it.

Also grabbed a frozen pizza. Been craving it, for some reason. Just seems to be on my mind a lot lately.

And... and Dick's pancake. Pizza. Cannabis. Jake. Huh— am I missing something, here?

Can't be. Just, the timing, right? It's... uncanny.

Shook the thought out of my stupid bloody paranoid head. Too much of them true crime audiobooks I listen to on the road, keeping me awake on duty. Still, I—

"Mr Paul?" Jayir asked, as I stood fecklessly at the counter.

"Bloody hell, sorry, mate. Here," I said, tapping the plastic. "Seeya."

He smiled as I trotted out the door, back home. Leave her choccies on the side table, next to her chair. Sure she'll like that. We can share the pizza for tea, if she decides to eat with me, that is. Stranger things have happened—like a Dick pancake day after he told me about a druggie pizza.

Honestly, what is wrong with me? This is bloody Wisbech, not some action movie. It was an accident, plain as day—I found the bloke, and I'm sure of that.

I settled into the sofa, pulling out my phone. Email gone out from the head honcho himself, it seems. Let's have a look then:

Dear Employees,
We are sorry to announce the tragic passing of Dick Richards, sadly from an agricultural accident late last night, confirmed by police and ambulatory crew. Employees are reminded to be wary of heavy machinery whilst lone working, and call Paul or Jake for mobile support.
Condolences,
Mark Holland, CEO and owner Securoguard Services

Chest felt tight staring at it. Whole man's life, came down to one sodding moment where he wandered a bit too close to a bloody harvester. What was he even doing there? Shortcut, maybe? His rounds wouldn't have taken him past it, so he was cutting corners to get back to the hut faster. Makes sense—bloody freezing out there this time of year.

Brief smile flickered on my face. McNology. Think you would have liked improv, Dick. Dedicate my next skit to you, mate. Bloody hell, not starting with these waterworks again. Wasn't like he was my best mate, so why am I being such a big girl about it?

Wait a minute, Dick Richards? So his full name is Richard Richards? His dad had a bloody sense of humour on him then!

Felt my eyes betray me, closing, falling into slumber on the sofa. Best get... best rest.

Bloody hell. Open my eyes, sound of the front door closing. Mary home already then?

"What's this?" she asked, picking up those awful plastic shells I bought her.

"Yours."

"Thanks," she said, shrugging, slumping into her armchair. Not sure why I bother sometimes.

I could say something. Maybe ask her why she's being such a grouch. Maybe ask her to just dance with me, in the living room, like we used to. Think that cat outside might like to join outside? Ginger tabby one. Cute fella.

I sighed. Well, least she said thanks. But no, look at her, Paul—really, look at her. She's... nervous. Look at her face. Not even reaching for wine, not even turning the telly on. Just sat there, frowning.

"Mary, you alright, love?" I asked.

She stared at me for what felt like a small eternity. At me, or through me, I couldn't tell. Still—I know my wife. Something isn't right.

"No," she stated, finally. Pulled out her phone, hand shaking a little. I groaned, knees moaning at me as I stood up to go see.

"Bloody kids," I muttered, seeing the photo she took. Bag of weed, hidden behind the lockers at the school.

Mary sighed. "Left it there. Didn't know what to do."

I shrugged. "It's been bloody everywhere lately, Mary. Car stinks of it on Monday. Bloody stoners."

"Will I be in trouble, Paul? Do I need to report it to someone?"

She seemed genuinely concerned, bless her, like she'd never seen a bag of weed before. Clearly forgot our late teens. Probably all that sodding wine.

"I know a teacher who works there. See him on Fridays, at improv. Want me to tell him?"

That was a practical, pragmatic solution I felt. I let him know, he takes care of it, Mary doesn't have to admit to seeing it. Nice and simple, professional.

"I don't know, Paul. Should we really get involved at all? Seemed like it was left there for someone and I—"

"Don't stress, love," I interrupted. "Hey, do you want something nice to think about? Take your mind off it?"

Mary seemed to give the idea some pause, her face written with uncertainty. "Yeah. Yeah, I would, Paul."

"I know it's not really your thing, love, but—"

I regaled her with tales from improv club. Space sailors, flying around the moon. Interdimensional cheesecakes. Dragon egg omelettes. The degree in McNology. That ginger tabby cat outside.

For the first time in years, I found myself genuinely enjoying talking. She really seemed to be listening to me, too—might even have chuckled at that degree. Damnit, Dick—you'd have loved improv club. Clumsy git. Pancaked prat. Sigh.

"Well, not my thing, Paul. But sounds like you had fun."

Her smile warm, genuine. I felt my frown curling up, too.

"Oh, I bought us a pizza for dinner. Little bit of a telly date together, what do you say?" I said, chest feeling tight.

"Sorry, Paul. Soaps tonight," Mary deflected.

Ah well. Can't say I didn't try. "Righto. I'll be in the study," I said, shuffling off, before stopping dead in my tracks at the door.

Bags of weed in a pizza box. Bag of weed in the locker room, at school. Jake. Dick pancake.

Is... is this connected? It's—it's a lot of coincidences in a short space of time. I—does the cheesecake have something to do with this? It had to, how else could this—

"Paul? You alright?" Mary asked, seeing me hover in the hallway.

"Sorry, love. Just musing. Off I go then. Pizzas and pancakes."

She didn't reply. I shuffled off back to my study, digging through for a book to read. Somehow, I found myself dreading that frozen pizza for dinner. It was flat. Flat as a pancake.

Chapter 7 - Pizzas and Pancakes

Taking Wednesday off didn't seem to help me any, really. If I'm going to be up all night anyway, might as well be doing my rounds. Time to call the other ball and chain.

"Mark Holland, Securoguar—"

"Hey, Mark, it's Paul. I'm fine, mate, eager to get back to work," I said, meaning every word. Probably.

"Ah, hi, Paul. You sure you're alright to? You found Dick only—"

"You know me, mate, ever the professional," I interrupted. None of this touchy-feely stuff please, Mark, I might mistake you for actually giving a shit. *Sorry to hear that.*

"So, as it happens, I've already got Jake to cover for you tonight. But listen, Paul, something I want to talk to you about," he began.

Here we bloody go again, another age discrimination tale coming my way. Enough with the pause then, Mark, let me hear it. Bloody farm again, I bet.

"Ahem... well, as it happens, we *do* have need of a new static guard at the farm," he continued. "Not age discrimination, I can assure you Paul."

Have need of a new guard? Dick pancaked a couple of days ago, and he "has need of a new guard." I shouldn't feel slighted by him pointing out the obvious, but I gripped my phone tighter all the same.

"You've less than a decade till retirement, Paul. I'd like to promote you to sta—"

"No thanks," I cut him off, like a pair of scissors through a cheesecake. "Quite happy on my rounds. Can't sit still all night, Mark."

"Look, before you say no," he began once more.

What's he going to do to sweeten the deal this time then? More money? Ten minutes with his Swedish model wife every weekend? Trip to the moon?

Moon actually seemed more likely than the money or the model, to be honest.

"Sorry, Mark, I missed that, mate. But I'm already quite happy on—"

"Look, Paul, it suits a business need for me. It suits you, too, your knackered old knees. Be honest with yourself for once, mate. More money too, like I said."

My knackered old knees could still knock you out, you prick. Bloody discrimination—no need for it, is there.

"Mark, I'm not going static."

He sighed audibly through the phone. Not very professional of you, Mark.

"Paul, I've worked with you a long time. Consider you a friend, even. Integral part of Securoguard. But—"

"I tell you what, Mark," I snapped. "I'll give you one night a week at that bloody farm. But rest I'm in my car, alright?"

I could almost hear his cogs turning, as the echo of his fingers drumming the desk came through the line.

"Yeah, I can work with that. I'm moving you to farm Monday, mobile Tuesday to Thursday. Jake is taking Friday to Monday on mobile. Sound?"

I wanted to argue, really. Let the stupid stoner take one of my shifts, might be opening up Pandora's bloody box here. But I was tired. So, so tired. Really need you to let me get some sleep, Dick.

"Fine, Mark. Farm Mondays, but I'm mobile rest of the week."

"Deal. Farm Monday, mobile Tuesday to Thursday. Well, I'll give Jake the route tonight still, if you fancy a headstart on the farm?"

No I bloody don't. Paul pancake. Christ, how am I gonna work there, thinking about it? Bloody hell.

"No, mate. I'll just stay off then," I muttered, deflated, defeated.

"Great, great. Bye Paul."

Call ended with a click. I sighed, still sprawled out in bed, still tired but not sleepy. Guess I'll drag you knackered old bones out of here, get dressed, find something to do.

Didn't fancy whittling away the day in the study, somehow. Felt more like a weekend thing. Could cook that frozen pizza—never did have it last night.

Josh and his pizza box, hoarding it away from me like a dragon sat atop a pile of gold, popped into my head. His face—what was wrong with it? Hungry? Or scared?

What am I missing, here? Bloody hell, my stupid knees hurt, I thought as I pulled on my clothes. Stared at myself in the mirror a long while. Grey as a pigeon, wrinkled as a raisin, green eyes lost their spark. Seems like ten minutes ago I was young, fit, fast. Time flies.

Shook the thoughts from my head, and headed to the kitchen. Cup of tea, that'll perk me right up. I can already smell it steeping.

I'll call Mary. Maybe she wants to have lunch.

Voicemail—bugger. I tap my fingers on the kitchen table, waiting for the tea to cool, but when had I made it? Eyelids feeling heavy, can barely pry them open now. Breathing slow, rhythmic. In, out. In.

Several hours later, I stir from the armchair as light bombards my eyes. I don't even recall getting here. The lights are blinking, on and off, on and off. My breathing heavy, click click click—Mary?

"Wake up, sleepyhead," she said, flicking the light switch off and on again. "You're in my spot."

Bloody hell. Not very kind, Mary.

"Ugh... what time is it?" I asked gently, rubbing my tired eyes.

"Gone six. I didn't want to wake you, but I'm missing my soaps."

Well, can't be having that now, can we. I'm sure whatever Vera did whilst drunk with Phil is very bloody interesting. Can't think about that much longer, I'll doze off again.

Knees protested, pushing myself up from my chair. Least my arms have never failed me.

"Enjoy, love," I said, shuffling out the way. "Need anything?"

"No, thanks," she mumbled, fidgeting in her armchair. Well, least I warmed it up for her.

Off to my study, I lose myself in a book. Finally caught your white whale, now don't know what to do with yourself. Poor bastard.

Hours pass, and no matter how hard I try, I can't distract myself. A merry-go-round of pancakes and pizzas, dancing a circle in my head.

Dick tried to tell me something before he became a pancake, though, didn't he? Can't be related, police ruled it an accident. But didn't he seem a little off? The pizza and the weed bags. Bloody stoner.

Still—I'm not in work tonight, am I. School isn't exactly far, and I can grab myself some fast food after, can't I? Unless I catch tubby with another pizza, of course—and this time, he's sharing with me.

This isn't professional. This is me curious, wanting to see what the bloody hell is going on. Connecting dots that don't exist because I'm bored, stressed, and trying to escape the ghosts in my brain.

Honestly though, why not. Nothing better to do, Mary busy with her soaps, no kids to check in with. Can only re-read Moby Dick so many times.

Pull on my coat, grab my keys, hand on the door.

"Heading out, Mary. Need anything?"

"More red. Love you."

More wine. Course you do. Fine, I'll play along. All gotta die of something, don't we—your liver, your choice, isn't it.

"Will do, love. Enjoy your cakes."

She didn't reply. Too busy with Vera and Phil and all the others I can't bring myself to give a shit about. Well, off I go then. Did I say cakes or soaps? Same thing.

Sat in my car, trusty, rusty Fiat so old I could probably slap her in a museum. Quick visit to my good man at the corner shop, two bottles of red, and a cup of coffee for me. Think this stuff'll be what does me in—still, preferable to a Paul pancake.

Keep the wine in the footwell, make sure it's safe. Wrap it in my jacket—that'll do. Short drive to get to the school in Wisbech. Private one, quite posh in fact—amazed Mary found a baggie here. Especially with Josh watching the place overnight too.

Unless he's a smoker too, of course. Could explain the weight problem, maybe he gets the munchies.

But he just never struck me as the type. Met all sorts across my many decades on this big blue ball, and I just know it ain't his bag.

So why is this still nagging at me? Am I about to watch a kid get a pizza and demand a slice, really? And for what? Pride? Professionalism? Pizza?

I sighed, pulled up down the street. I can see the school entrance from here, but the kid can't see me. I drove past first, naturally, just to make sure he's there.

I've already made the effort to come here, so I'll see this through. Besides, got Dick haunting me anyway. Sat over my shoulder, nagging me about pizza and stoners.

What am I gonna do if I catch him smoking on the job anyway? I ain't Mark. Can't really do anything but give him a bollocking. Maybe gather some evidence, report it to Mark myself? Let him know these kids are ruining the professional reputation of his business.

No more than his stupid bloody logo, I thought, seeing my work motor pull in. Jake the stoner, is it? Odd. Something just isn't sitting right with me here.

I drum my fingers across the steering wheel, waiting for him to leave. Doesn't take him long—two, three minutes tops. He's all business, edge like a letter opener.

Right, he's pulled off now. My turn.

Feel my heart beating a samba approaching the guard hut. Looks bloody feckless—guess he don't recognise the motor.

Out he comes, shining a torch at me. More blinding than those bloody headlamps.

"Hello? Who's there?" he calls out, as I step out of my car, knees be damned.

"Well it ain't bloody Santa Claus, is it, mate?" I say, grin on my face.

Kid laughs, lowering his torch beam. "Paul! You alright, mate?" he says, sounding happy to see me.

Smile soon fades from his face as I approach him, though. Box of pizza, right there, this time dropped off by Jake no doubt. Bloody stoners.

"Wha—what are you doing here, Paul?" he asked, shiftily. Couldn't tell—was his tone accusatory or scared? Both, maybe? He had something in there, I was sure of it. Maybe even pancakes.

"Well, thought you might give an old man a slice of pizza, youngin. Respect your elders and all that," I replied with a grin.

His face painted a picture more beautiful than any Dickasso. You're up to something, kid, and your poker face ain't getting you very far in Vegas. Snake eyes.

"I—uh—that's just garlic bread," he stammered.

Garlic bread? He'd last four minutes at improv. Christ, kid. Sweating like a pig, flapping around like a fish out of cola—what's he bloody well up to here?

"Well, all the same to me, mate. Open up, give us a slice."

"No! I don't—you can't make me—"

"Open it," I decreed, arms folded. "Or do I call Mark right now? Maybe the old bill?"

His lip was quivering now. Not sure exactly what I've caught him doing, but it's not something good—he's made that clear just with his face. What the bloody hell is he up to then? Does this have something to do with Dick pancake? Are pancakes illegal now?

"Don't. Please. You're not even on tonight, Paul, why are you here—"

"Last chance," I declared, phone out, unlocked and ready.

"Stop! OK! I'll talk!" he yells, sobbing like a schoolgirl. Christ's sake, Josh, be a man. My dad would have clobbered you for that. Not very professional.

I follow him into the hut, pizza box sat on the side. His hand visibly trembling as he places it on the lid.

"Please just go, Paul. I don't—"

"Open it."

Seemed I was done playing games. Sorry, kid, I've a duty to see this through now—you're hiding something and it's time you showed me.

He sighed, lifting the lid quickly on the pizza box before shutting it again. Just like Dick said—bags of cannabis attached to the lid. Great—another bloody stoner.

No. Wait.

I glared at him, stood in silence. He opened his mouth a few times as if to speak, but no words came. Dick. Pizza. Cannabis. Mary.

Two kids, both stoners. But are they? Look at him. Kid's never smoked a joint in his life. Coiled up so tight, when he finally gets a girlfriend I think he might just explode. Kid doesn't know how to relax.

45

He's bloody moving it, making himself a few quid on the side. Josh, and Jake, and that other delivery guy too. Worse still? Using a bloody school. Bastards.

Clenched my fists tight, glaring at him harder. Felt the rage building in my chest. One thing to smoke a little weed—we were all young and dumb once.

But these little bastards are busy flogging it. Jake delivers it, Josh hides it, someone sells it. He attended this posh git school, didn't he—must be someone younger, still here. Probably in sixth form.

Right then. Time for a calm, professional chat.

"You're bloody flogging weed here, aren't you?" I angrily accused Josh, as he stood there feckless.

"Paul, I swear," he mumbled. "I just take it, leave it behind the lockers, take my bonus. I'm not involved."

"That's literally the definition of involved, you stupid fuck! You're drug dealing!"

"No! No, I just leave it! I don't—"

I shook my head. "Fooled yourself, kid, but not me. Mark won't be fucking happy. Police either. So Jake delivers it?"

"No, I swear! It's the Spicy Pizza Palace place, he just brought it for me! He's got no idea, please don't tell him, please!"

He was begging, practically grovelling at this point. No dignity in the kid whatsoever. Christ.

"Bloody hell. Well he ain't stupid, so does he smoke it or—"

"He isn't involved! Don't talk to him, please! Or Mark!"

Why was he so bloody terrified? I mean, there's enough weed there for him to lose his job. Maybe a short suspended sentence—but I doubt he'd see jail over this. I need him to talk—this is getting weird now. Not the cathartic catch-a-clown I'd envisioned.

Look at his face, Paul. He's blubbering like a bloody whale, scared shitless. Ah. I got it.

"First time you been in trouble, is it, mate?" I asked gently.

"Yeah. Yeah, it is," he sobbed.

Bless him. Bloody idiot. What am I gonna do here?

I sighed, staring at him as he composed himself. His face was red, eyes finally stopped leaking but puffy and bloodshot. Need to sort this out with him, be professional.

"Right. You're done with this little game, you hear me? And I want to know what's going on. You've clearly been at this a while, kid. Now why?"

He slumped into his chair, fluorescent light in the hut buzzing harshly above us as the bright light battled against the darkness.

"The takeaway place makes pizzas, then—look, I swear, I just place the bags and take the money. That's all I do, nothing else! I promise!"

Bloody hell. Can't just turn a blind eye to this, can I? Kid has prospects. He's saving for uni, I know he is—told me so himself. For fuck's sake, Paul. Just be professional. Do the right thing.

"You're done doing it. But I want names, I want locations, I want everything. Everything, kid."

I'll keep him out of it—for now. Kid's just a pawn, dumb kid who needed money for uni. Bloody idiot. Shouldn't be messing with pancakes and pizzas at his age. Clearly doesn't know they're illegal now.

"I don't know—"

"Not good enough," I interrupted. "Spill it, kid."

He looked around the hut a while, as if a leprechaun was going to pop out of his pizza box and wish me away. Sorry, kid, not going anywhere.

"Look," he said finally. "I don't know that stuff—but if you'll leave me out of it, I can find out for you. Deal?"

I considered it for a long moment. Obviously, this has to go to Mark one way or another—but if I keep the kid out of

47

it, maybe he still has a chance. Think I've put the fear of bloody Dick pancake in him tonight, bless him.

"Right. I'm giving you a chance, then. I'll be back tomorrow night, start of your shift, before my improv club. See you then," I said, walking out and leaving the blubbering kid to his weed pizza.

Breathed deep, getting back into my car and driving home. Sorry I didn't hear you, Dick—but at least I sorted it now. Bloody harvester. Well, wife's waiting—let's get this wine home, but first? Think I'll take the long way back. Drive past the Bear's Paw, make sure I don't see Darren on the door. Sorry wifey, your wine can wait.

Chapter 8 - Just a bit of Weed

Slept a little better that night, truth be told, though ghosts still haunt me. Felt good though, giving a kid a second chance like that. I guess sometimes the right thing, and the professional thing are at odds with one another.

But discretion and experienced judgement matter. Mark doesn't want me to bother him with every little detail—too busy raking it in, paying me pennies on the pounds he's charging. I do the job, he just profits from it. Prick.

Still, Friday again. Improv night. Yet... I wasn't smiling. Just kept thinking about Dick, squashed like a bloody pancake under that harvester. He'd have fit in like a glove.

Hannah sells the things, doesn't she. Wouldn't it be tragic, ironic even, if she sold the farm that particular one. Would that technically make her a murderer?

I laughed out loud, staring up at the ceiling. Sorry, Dick—you knew I liked my dark humour. Still, if you can do me a favour and stop appearing under my eyelids, I would appreciate it, mate. Let an old man get a proper rest.

Not like the one you're now having, though. Not yet anyway. Work to do, rounds to make, then take Mary on a bloody cruise or something. Light a firework under this marriage.

That'll be the bloody day. More likely to fund her a private liver transplant than a cruise. Bloody hell.

Still, can't lie here moping all day. Time to kill before improv, and—oh right. I'm off to school first, see that bloody kid and find out what he knows. There are certain things Mark does need to know about, and I'm giving him something. If not Josh, maybe that stoner bastard Jake?

Come to think of it, why did Josh profess his innocence? What did he say, Paul? Think!

Nah. He didn't say anything important, not really. But he was scared—I still don't really understand it. Was he eating pancakes? No, he said he only eats fatty things now. Probably.

Shook the thoughts from my head, headed to the kitchen. Cup of tea, that'll calm the nerves. Mary already left—think she's cleaning the pub today, not really sure. Don't need to know, do I.

Sat with my tea, listening to the chirping birds. Almost forgot what a robin sounded like, rare as a spotted tiger these days.

My turn for the telly, then. Let's see what passes for cooking these days. Now Mary could bloody cook, back when she gave a shit—swear I married her for her Sunday roast. Probably been a decade since we had one. I wonder if that harvester gathered the wheat making the flour used for the Yorkshire puddings? It was all connected. Probably.

Several hours passed, and after a long staring contest had with the telly I found my eyelids heavy again. Couldn't let myself fall asleep, though—time for school.

Felt important picking out a nice outfit for the occasion, somehow. I couldn't put my finger on why—I'm off to go interrogate a kid, not a date with Mrs Holland.

Really should drop that. I'm happily married. Well, married anyway. Besides, I don't actually fancy her—think I just like the idea of getting one over on Mark. Some people just need to feel small in their lives, even if only for a few minutes. Bet she would look good driving that harvester though.

Nice black polo shirt and trousers. Almost look like a golfer, though my knees would never allow that. Well, knees and income, anyway. Maybe Josh could go golfing, all that extra weed money he's making. Help him shift the rest of the blubber, too.

I hopped in my car, headed over to school. He'd be in the hut by now, and I'd have time to chat to him before improv. Should have bought him some pancakes, though—where were my bloody manners?

As I pull into the school, can't help but notice his car is gone. That red Toyota—that's Claire?

Pull up at the hut, hop out. She's stepped out to greet me already.

"Paul? What are you doing here?"

"Hello, Claire. Where's Josh?"

"Quit."

Bloody hell. Quit? But that's—that doesn't make any—

Clenched my fists, breathing deep. Bloody hell, kid, what did you go and do? I bet he took that bloody pizza with him too, didn't he? He still owes me a slice!

"Paul?" Claire asked, staring at me.

"Oh, right. Sorry. Was meant to speak to him here. So you're covering for him, then."

"Yeah. I'm a cover guard, remember. Mark said he's fucked off to Newcastle."

Bloody hell. That's half a country away, near Scotland. Did I scare the poor kid off? I wasn't that intimidating, was I? Scratched the back of my neck, staring at Claire. Still plastered in bloody makeup, ready for her ratwalk.

"Paul," Claire boomed, bloody loud as always. Seriously, doesn't this girl have an inside voice? "Are you alright? You look pale."

"I'm fine," I deflected. None of this touchy-feely crap, please and thank you. Not professional. "Do you have his number or something?"

Claire shrugged. "Nope. He owe you money or something, Paul? You seem upset."

51

"I'm fine," I parroted. Apparently she didn't hear me the first time. Probably deafened herself, that bloody loud booming voice of hers. "Well, have a good night, Claire. I'm off to improv club."

"Improv club? What's that then?" she asked, grin on her face.

Brushed my polo shirt, staring at her. Ah, what the hell. Dick liked it, maybe she will, too.

"Oh, so, you pretend. You make up these scenarios, and you have some fun with it. Silly really, all just daft. Want to try it?"

She chuckled, chest heaving as she did. "Why not. What do we do?"

Hmm. Let's think. Sailors? Dragon eggs? Cheesecakes? Oh! I got it.

"We're married, looking to buy a house together. But it's visibly haunted by ghosts."

Claire laughed out loud, echoing through my ears as she did. "Brilliant! So, how do we do this?"

Cleared my throat. "Well, love, we pay the owners a lot of money then it's ours. But that lady in a dress keeps flying between the walls? You're seeing that, right?"

"Oh! Yes! This place is haunted. Everyone knows that," Claire said.

"Is it all inclusive? Do they come with the purchase price, do you think?" I followed.

"Wonder if they increase the property value?" Claire chimed in.

"Good question. I'll ask the realtor, when he flies back in here himself!"

Claire and I chuckled a little. Daft, but a welcome distraction from the ghosts beneath my heavy eyelids.

"Well, seems interesting, Paul, though I'm not sure it's my thing. Did make me laugh though. Thanks," Claire said with a smile.

"Yeah. Was going to be Dick's first session tonight," I admitted. "Bloody pancake."

Claire visibly frowned. "Yeah. Poor bastard. Email from Mark came across a bit callous, didn't it?"

Felt my frown curling upwards. "Exactly! Bloody reminder of safety procedures, day after Dick gets pancaked."

Claire narrowed her gaze. "Right. Well, seeya later then, Paul."

Made her way back into the hut, shutting the door. That was odd—probably late for her next ratwalk. Guess I'll head to improv, then.

Pulled into the car park, Hannah already here as expected. Rain or shine, nuclear war or zombie apocalypse she was always here first. Oh—and Stephen was here, too. Nice to see him on time for once. No sign of the Simons yet though, not even the fictional one.

"Hi, Paul!" Hannah announced loudly, sat next to Stephen, seeing me shuffle in. Coffee and cheap floor polish lingered in my eyes once more.

"Hello both. How are we?" I asked, shaking the image of Dick from my mind once more. Guess he's coming to his first improv after all, just this time as a bloody pancake ghost.

"We're both fine, aren't we, Stephen?" Hannah said cheerily. He just shrugged his shoulders, glaring at the floor. Miserable sod. "But how are you, Paul?" she continued, grin wide, kindness in her eyes.

"Oh, you know. Fine as shandy," I remarked, trailing off as Dick popped back into my head. Come on, mate, give an old man some peace already—I come here to forget about reality, not force myself into it.

Hannah squeezed my shoulder, offering me a smile. Somehow, seemed to know I needed the humanity. Kind woman—no idea why she's not found herself a husband yet. Though I had to admit, the way she looks at Stephen, maybe there's a tea brewing there. Or a relationship.

More people trickled in, including Tom. Poor bugger was late, lumping himself with the wonky chair. Somehow, he made even that seem straight as an edge.

One warmup later, all the bloody zips and boings—honestly, need something new. Tired of that. Time to play now, though.

"Let's get a prompt volunteer. How about you, Paul?" Hannah suggested.

Fine. I'll play along. Think, Paul, think.

"Uh, let's see. You're a ghost trying to order a pizza from Stephen?"

Hannah chuckled loudly. "Bizarre. Well, I do fancy a pizza, but I can't press these bloody buttons!" she said, mimicking her hand going right through an invisible phone.

"Hold on," Stephen said, "if you can't call me, how can I deliver you a pizza?"

Hannah shook her head. "Come on, Stephen. Play ball. Yes, and."

Stephen sighed, clenching his fist. Bloody hell, almost looked like he wanted to sock her one. He alright? Not very professional for a teacher.

"I'm sick of dealing with your bloody pizzas, you stupid bi—ghost." Stephen snapped.

"Well, I'm the customer, aren't I, sweetie? And I'm hungry, so get me that pizza!"

Bloody hell. Could cut the tension in here with a knife. Something must be going on between these two? I scratched my chin, studied them both. He's divorced, she's single—hmm. There's subtext, here, fairly sure of that now.

"I can't deliver your bloody pizza, I don't know how!" Stephen protested.

"Oh come on, dear. Where's the yes, and? You're a smart guy. Think of a way. I'm a ghost, you could séance. Or a Ouija board. Maybe off yourself, come have a chat?"

Stephen stormed out. Bloody hell—what the hell was that all about?

"Sorry, everyone," Hannah said frowning. "I seem to have upset him somehow—someone go make sure he's alright in a minute please."

She seemed as confused as the rest of us. Are they shagging? Not the only one seeing the subtext, I'm sure. Look at the faces, especially Tom. Best do something, Hannah, get control back.

"Paul, you up for the challenge?" she said, smiling at me.

"Oh, let's give it a go then. If my bloody old knackered knees let me."

Few chuckles from the crowd. "You should try being a ghost like me, Paul—I just fly everywhere!"

"Does sound bloody nice. Right then... I summon the spirit of Hannah Rogers! Hear my call and answer my questions. I got my Ouija board right here."

She gently grabbed my hand, her skin soft and cold to the touch. Mimicked moving my hand across the invisible letters.

"Let's see," I started. "P... I... Z... Z again? A? She wants a pizza! Right, well I just so happen to have one here. You want extra ectoplasm with that?"

Chuckles from the crowd, Hannah patting my shoulder. "Well done, Paul. That was fun. Next, please?"

There you go, Dick. Think you'd have enjoyed that one. Maybe I should head out front, see if Stephen is alright.

Shuffled out front, found him slumped in a plastic chair, arms folded.

"There you are, mate," I said, sitting beside him. Bloody hell, does he look miserable. Knackered wasn't even the word—maybe cream crackered?

"What do you want, Paul?" he asked, folding his arms tighter. Don't you get defensive with me, sunshine.

"Just wanted to see you were alright. You got a little hot there," I gently suggested.

He sighed, arms moving to his knees. "Yeah. Sorry. Just a lot of stress on at the school."

Oh right! He works at that bloody school. Teacher. Mary, Josh and the bloody Hufflepuff stuff.

"Ah, been meaning to talk to you about that, actually," I began. He visibly frowned, locking eyes with me. Christ, almost looked like he wanted to cry, poor bastard. "My wife cleans there part-time, as you know. Well, my Mary found a bit of Mary Jane behind the lockers, if you know what I mean."

He looked away, clenched his fists. Didn't like hearing that, it seemed.

"Why tell me?" he asked, cold and curt.

"You teach there, silly. Thought you'd want to know?"

Not bloody rocket science, is it, mate? Wake up, Stephen. Looks as tired as I feel, I swear. Do I tell him about Josh too? Or that ginger tabby cat? Maybe not.

"Right, I see. Did you tell anyone else, Paul?" he asked.

"Not yet. Figured I'd just let you know. Bloody kid there was dealing it, but he's fucked off to Newcastle! Overnight, just like that. Bloody ridi—Stephen?"

He began to hyperventilate, his body shaking as he breathed rapidly. Bloody hell, not very professional this— and all over a bit of bloody weed. How the hell does he manage a room full of teenagers?

"Stephen, mate? You alright?"

He breathed deep and long, visibly trying to calm himself down.

"Fine, Paul. Sorry, just a lot to take in."

"Just a bit of bloody weed, mate. Not the end of the world, is it?"

He narrowed his gaze, clenching his fists again. "No. No, I don't suppose it is, is it. You're right, Paul. Just a bit of weed. Well, thanks for letting me know."

"Course, mate. You coming back in there then?" I asked, patting him on the shoulder.

"Yeah. Let's go have some fun," he said, as we made our way back inside to the zips and the boings and the pizza pancake ghosts. Time for a bit of fun then.

Chapter 9 - Star Witness

I've grown to loathe these weekends, in all honesty. I've come to a bit of a realisation—I judge Mary, sitting there with her soaps and her wines—but am I any better?

I look around me, staring at my books as I'm stood in the doorway of my study. Every wall shelved, every shelf full—yet I still keep buying more of the bloody things, piling them up in front.

There are worse habits, I know—could be into drugs, or pancakes, or bloody gambling. Christ, fuck that.

But a vice is a vice, and I read. No, not even that is it—look at these bloody shelves, Paul. I've read dozens of books, but there's hundreds of them in here. How many times have I read Of Mice and Men, yet To Kill a Mockingbird has sat gathering dust? I don't even know what it's about.

Still, it's Monday now, and I can't be arsed with all this bloody introspection. Young man's game, that. I'm clearly just tired, ghost of Dick still fucking hovering under my eyelids. Piss off already, mate—not like we were best friends, is it. I need to sleep and you aren't letting me.

Felt my chest heave, sighing. Guess I better get ready, head down to the office, pick up my keys. Mary should be there cleaning today, actually—might stop in and give her a hug.

Hands on the wheel, focusing on the road as I drive through Leverington. Must admit, even a cranky old git like me enjoys the scenery here. Trees overhang the road as I approach Wisbech. All so flat, like the rest of the fens. The hills aren't alive with the sound of anything here—there aren't bloody any.

Pull up in the yard, office blazing bright in the twilight, sun setting across the horizon. It all makes you feel a bit small, fully taking it in.

But where's my bloody motor then? No ugly Securoguard logo, no bloody smell of weed from that bloody stoner?

I waltz into the office, seeing Mary bent over the desk, buffing away. Mark stood behind her, ploughing her from behind, slapping of skin on skin as he nails my wife like a hammer.

Violently shake the image from my head, nearly retching. He's sat in his office, on his phone as usual. Smile to the wife, cleaning away as she should be. Bloody imagination. Ah well, gives me a break from your gormless mug, don't it, Dick.

"Hey, love," I say to Mary, her offering me a slight smile as I approach. Mark offers me a casual wave from his office, still on that bloody phone.

"Hi, Paul. I'm about done here now. See you tomorrow," Mary states, packing up her supplies.

"Righto. I'll talk to the boss man. Love you."

"You too," she mumbles, heading off. Date with the wine and soaps, no doubt.

"Paul? What are you doing here?" Mark asked, poking his head out his office door. "You've a shift at the farm in—"

Oh bollocks. No wonder my bloody car isn't here— stoner boy has it. Forgot I'd agreed to this bollocks. Sigh.

"Paul? You OK, mate?" Mark said, eyebrows raised.

"What? Oh, right. Sorry, Mark, I almost forgot. I'll head there now, but—"

Cut myself off, looking at his face. Bloody hell, I've a professional responsibility, don't I. Can't just bottle this stuff up—I'd best pipe up. Pizzas and pancakes.

"Josh alright? I'm worried about him. Look, Mark, I caught him with a bag of weed."

Mark raised an eyebrow. "Cannabis?"

"Yeah. He was leaving it there for someone and getting a bit of bonus money from it, he said."

Mark beckoned me into his office. Best follow, I thought, shuffling after him as he sat down.

"What did the kid say exactly?" Mark asked.

"Oh, didn't seem too serious, Mark. Seems like him and Jake got some weed thing going on there. Jake smokes it, I'm sure of that. Bloody stoner."

Mark nodded. "Yeah. I remember you complaining about the smell before. Did you call the police?" he stated, sharp as a cheesecake.

"No, boss. I figure it might hurt the business, no sense getting the old bill involved over a few tea leaves, is it?"

Mark sighed, pocketing his mobile. Seemed pleased to hear that—guess it makes sense, could hurt his reputation if a thing like that got out. Unprofessional.

"Right, Paul. Did you take any photos, evidence, tell anyone else?"

Ah, bloody hell. Didn't think to take a photo, did I. Bloody dinosaur, me.

"Sorry, Mark," I said, disappointed. "Didn't occur to me. I've let you down."

Mark sighed again. Guess I really did disappoint him this time. Stegosaurus. Wonder if a stegosaurus would eat pizza? Probably.

"No, no, don't worry, Paul. Thanks for bringing it to me. Let me handle it—put it behind you, have a good night down at the farm. Call if you need me, alright?"

Calm down there, Mark. Sometimes, it almost seems like you give a shit. I'm in danger of thinking you have feelings

61

beyond covetousness. You and your bloody money, Mark. Be the death of you, I'm sure. Loves cash like it'll love him back, the muppet.

"Yeah, will do. Sorry again, Mark. See you," I said, shuffling out the door. Right then—guess I'm taking old trusty rusty here down the farm, then. The farm where less than a week ago a harvester made a Dick pancake. Fuck.

I gripped the wheel tight on my way to the farm. Why were my sodding hands shaking? Getting old bloody sucks.

Pulled up, parked in the same spot Dick always did. Should I move? What if—well, he ain't exactly going to bloody well need it now, is he?

My legs felt like jelly getting out the car. Bloody old aching knees, causing me grief. Well, into the guard hut with me, I s'pose.

Oh come on now, this is pathetic. Who's been watching this site with Dick gone? They've left his bloody cup of tea on the side, curdled and horrible. So bloody unprofessional.

I chucked that right out, down the dyke nearby. Let the murky water carry it away. Fuck it, and the mug too. Go get buried by sludge and muck, you bloody mug.

My chest felt tight. I was being unprofessional, I could feel it. I shouldn't bloody be here—my place is the road, in the motor, mobile patrol. That's why I'm so worked up—this is age discrimination, plain and simple.

I settled in, ready for my first patrol. That bloody harvester, still here, but they bolted the rotary bit at the front back on now. Probably tightened those bolts to within an inch of their life this time. Sat there staring at me like he hadn't just made a Dick pancake. I was the Michelin tyre chef here, not you, bloody harvester.

If anyone gave a shit about health and safety the first time, Dick might not be a pancake right now. Bloody hell—felt my eyes leaking, staring at the harvester. Bloody cold wind, causing me tears. Best finish this patrol, get back inside.

Oh. They got some new containers. Well, new to this farm, anyway—rusted-up pieces of crap. Must be holding some expensive equipment, locked up like Fort bloody Knox. Oh, that or the fertiliser. Strict instructions for farms to keep that under lock and key now, especially since those terrorists made that bloody bomb on the news. Bastards.

Half hour or so later, back in the hut and buzz of the fluorescent light is doing my bloody head in. How the hell Dick put up with this, I'll never know. Ah, headlights—a visitor? A bloody thief? Aliens?

"Fenland Agricultural Machinery Sales", it said on the side, shining my torch at it. Bloody hell, that's the one what Hannah works at, she—bloody hell! That is Hannah!

"Hannah! What are you doing here?" I call out happily, her smiling on her approach.

"Paul, so lovely to see you outside of improv! I've worked for FAMS for years, I told you," she began. "Just here to assess a potential problem, that's all."

Bloody hell, Hannah. Too bad you didn't come a week ago, replace that shoddy old rustbucket harvester. Dick might still be here and not a pancake.

"Farmer know you're coming down?"

"Spot visit," she said quickly. "They want to replace the harvester, for some reason."

Not bloody surprised, after this old rustbucket cooked a Dick pancake. Doesn't she know? Should I tell her about it?

"Not surprised," I began. "Last guard got squashed under it like a tube of toothpaste."

Colour drained from her face, mouth agape. "Bloody hell! Sorry, Paul, excuse my French. That's horrific! What happened exactly?"

I sighed, replaying the events over in my mind once more. Stay still, stupid hands. Shake on your own time, I'm on the job here.

"Bloody hell," she said, after I finished explaining the Dick pancake situation. "That poor man."

"Hannah," I said, curling a frown upside down. "I know you like dark humour. Fancy a laugh?"

Hannah raised an eyebrow, smiling warmly. "Oh go on then. Let's hear it."

"Did you sell the farm this harvester?"

"I did, actually! Many moons ago now, Paul. Why?"

"Since it killed him, doesn't it technically make you a murderer?"

Colour drained from her face again. Eyes, narrowed, fixed, burrowing into my skull. Perhaps I was too professional in my delivery? Or—

She suddenly burst out laughing. "Oh my god! I suppose it does, doesn't it! Oh, that's hilarious, Paul! My god. You got me good there. Think a jury would move to convict?"

"Maybe, if they can get the harvester in as a witness?" I said, chuckling heartily myself.

Hannah was in stitches by this point. "Oh, oh my god, Paul. You have no idea how funny you are. Improv natural, I swear. Well, maybe we can move for a mistrial—don't think that thing will fit in the courtroom!"

Slapping my knackered old knees by this point, chest heaving with laughter. After the week, no month—who am I kidding here, YEAR I've bloody well had? I needed this laugh.

Hannah calmed herself, hand on my shoulder. Warm, soft and sweet as ever.

"Oh, Paul. I needed that laugh—thank you."

"Same here, love, was just thinking that myself. Oh, so you needed to check something?"

"Don't worry, I'm sure it's fine. I'll sell them that new harvester. But make sure we keep this one around, it's our star witness in my murder trial!"

Oh god, poor Dick, but I'm practically rolling with laughter at this point. Bloody needed that. Must have been hilarious, these tears escaping my eyes. Or maybe it was just cold.

"Friday can't come soon enough, Hannah. I'm excited already. Well, enjoy the rest of your night, dear."

"You too, Paul, take care. But stay away from that bloody harvester, it's a killer you know!"

"Oh Hannah, stop, please—my bloody ribs hurt!" I cackled between joyous laughter. So sorry, Dick, so sorry.

"See you, Paul!"

Ahh, I needed that. I smiled wide, waving her off as she left. Bit risky, me with the dark humour, but she loved it as much as I did. I'm glad. Well, guess I'm settling into my chair again. Got a mundane night of mud, tea, and stars ahead of me. Ghosts too.

Star bloody witness. Bloody hilarious.

Chapter 10 - Lamp through a Toaster

Glad to be done with that bloody farm. For this week, at least. Seems I'll have to be there every bloody Monday from now on.

Doesn't matter. Tuesday now, and I'm getting my car back. Bought another air freshener, too, from that happy chappy at the corner shop. Buy one every bloody week if I have to—money well spent.

Pulled up at the office. There she is, my motor. Bloody stupid logo. Oh, Mary's here too. Didn't she clean the place yesterday? Can't remember.

"Hi, love," I say, seeing her pop out of my patrol motor. It smelt bloody amazing—not a hint of the wacky baccy in my nose. Mary's doing?

"Oh, hey, Paul," she mumbles. "Got another hour's work, clean out Mark's car. Both the patrol cars, too."

Both? What bloody both? Just this one—that's all.

"Only the one, I thought? Boss man bought another one then?"

Mary nodded. "Yeah. His biggest earner, apparently."

My own wife knows more about the company I work for than I bloody do. Explain that one to me. Sodding Mark.

Made sense, though. He can charge clients two hours' pay for ten minutes of my time. I'm his biggest earner, no doubt. Well—except Jake, of course. Bloody stoner.

Hopped in my motor, waving to Mary as I do. She's not bothered, probably got her head in the soaps and wine already.

Think I'll vary the route up a little bit tonight. Keep it professional. Head past the Bear's Paw, make sure I don't see Dick there.

Or just stop in at the storage yard, which is before the bloody Paw. Christ, Paul. Get it together already. Bloody pancakes.

Pull into the yard, Darren—Dick? Darren sat in the guard hut. Rushes out his hut, straightens his jacket and stands to attention. Bloody hell, Darren, this ain't the military, mate. Calm down.

"Evening, mate," I say to Darren, groaning out me motor. "How's it going then?"

Let's get some answers from him. See what he's got to say for himself. Maybe he's seen the star witness himself?

"Evening, Paul. I uh—I've not done any more of, err, you know..."

Couldn't help but chuckle. Bloody hell, Darren. "Moonlighting, mate. That's the word you're looking for. That's all."

Darren smiles at me, though doesn't reach his eyes.

"Yeah... that. Paul, thanks again for that, you're a good—"

"Think nothing of it, end of story," I say, cutting him off like a fork through cheesecake. "How's the night then?"

"Been here two hours, and already bored out my bloody mind, mate," Darren admitted. Made sense, I s'pose—I knew where he was coming from after all night at the bloody farm. Those containers really did look the part—were they always there?

No, they brought them in after Dick became a pancake. I'm sure of it. Probably.

"Pancake? Paul?"

"Sorry, mate, off with the bloody aliens again," I say, chuckling.

"You, uh—you feeling alright, Paul?" Darren asked, staring at me a little too hard for my liking. Sorry, mate—you're not my type, and I'm hap—I'm married.

"Fine, mate. Why wouldn't I be?"

"You found Dick crushed under a harvester a week ago?"

My breathing, shallow, rapid. Eyes narrowed. Pulse in my ears.

Shook my head, breathed in deep.

"No big deal," I said. "Can't exactly inflate him back up like a balloon, can we now? Pancaked."

"Yeah, that's... that's... Paul?"

Oh bloody stupid knees. Fucking things. Turned to jelly, betrayed me, felt the cold harsh concrete beneath. Always knew they had it in for me, never trusted the bastards. Mutiny.

Dick offered me a hand. I grabbed it, Darren pulling me back to my feet. Darren, Darren, Darren.

"Sorry, Darren," I said, brushing myself off, "you get to my age your bloody knees betray you."

Darren put his arm round my shoulder. Honestly, not very professional, but I could use the help. Sat me down in his hut, spare chair from under the desk.

"I'll make you a cup of tea, Paul. Just sit a minute, mate," he said. Patronising git, I'm no bloody child. Tea does sound good, though.

"Thanks, mate."

I sigh, brushing off my legs again. Bits of bloody gravel stuck on my trousers. Bet I look a right silly sausage.

"So Claire told me about that little improv game you liked, Paul," Dick said. "Want to play with me? Sounded like a laugh, honestly."

Bloody hell. Is nobody a professional round here? All want to play their silly games, be daft, slack off. Job to do—that's all.

"Sure thing, Dick! I'll teach you," I said, Darren raising an eyebrow at me. What's got his goat then?

"Darren, mate. Called me Dick."

What? No I hadn't, I—did I? Slip of the tongue—that's all.

"So sorry, mate. On my mind, under my eyes, you know. Just a slip of the pancake. Right well, thanks for the tea. Best be—"

"You haven't drunk it yet, Paul," Dick said, pointing to my mug, my hands warming around it. Darren. Bloody hell, Darren, Darren, Darren.

Can people stop having such similar bloody names already? I'll call him William instead. That's much better.

"Sorry, mate, off with the aliens me," I chuckled. Tea tasted warm, inviting, just how I like it. He remembered I like one sugar. I never told him that, though, did I? Who could have told him? Bet it was the star witness. Bastard.

"Well, listen, William, I think you should call in sick," Darren said. "You've been through a lot, mate, seeing Dick get crus—"

"It's Paul, mate," I cut him off like a lamp through a toaster. "Well come on then, is it a uh... Darren?"

Darren seemed to be glowing now. A brilliant, bright, beautiful beacon in the darkness. Shining like a star, blazing like the sun, truly remarkable.

But where exactly the fuck am I? And who's this prick?

"He's coming to," the man in the green uniform said. "Can you hear me, sir?"

Green goblin seemed to be talking to me. I'd play along—why not?

"Fine, mate. Gotta go, got my patrol to—say, where's Dick?"

Darren stood by my side. "Paul, mate. You passed out, Dick is dead. Pancake, remember?"

Bloody hell. When did he become so patronising? Used to like the guy, even if he was a glowing bastard dancing in the moonlight.

I sat myself up, rubbed my eyes. Focus, Paul. Two green goblins, flashing blue lights, big colourful van—bloody ambulance or maybe a fire engine? What's all this then?

"Someone hurt?" I ask, now fully grasping the situation. Probably.

"Yes, mate, you had a fall. Passed out. Been over that, Paul," William said. He was getting on my nerves now.

Green goblin shined a little torch in my eyes. "Sir, have you been using drugs?" she asked.

What kind of stupid bloody question is that? That's the last thing I'd bloody do! Bloody ridiculous! She's a goblin, she should know pancakes are illegal.

"No," I stated plainly, like a plane soaring through the ocean. "Not since I was a teenager anyway, love. Was a year or two ago that!"

Chuckled away to myself, Dick looking concerned. Well, least I thought it was funny. I swear, nobody round here has a sense of humour. Bloody misers. Just trying to have a little fun, take my pancakes off my noodles.

Time passed. More time, still. Stood upon the hill, soaring by the brink. My head hurt, a lot, in fact. Perhaps my knees and head were working together? Mutiny, was it?

Woke up groggier than a pirate, back home, in my bed. Mary sat beside me, warm smile on her face. How'd I get here?

"Morning, sleepyhead," she said, kind, caring, compassionate. Mary? Bloody alien? What's all this then?

"Mary, I—"

"That's alright, Paul, get some rest. You collapsed on your shift. Is this about your friend?"

What friend? No seriously, I'm getting confused here.

"What do you mean?" I asked.

"You know, the uh... the farm? Your friend?"

Oh. Dick pancake. Why didn't she just say that. Hang on a minute—when did she start giving a shit?

"Not my friend. Just my colleague. Bloody pancake."

Mary frowned. "Well, I'm sure you miss him at improv club, Paul, and—"

Miss him? Never bloody went. Not like you go, either, is it, Mary. But bloody hell, all these people saying these things to me—is it time I really started paying attention? Listen to them?

I mean, think about it. When's the last time I've ever really, truly listened to someone without cutting them off, or—

"Do you agree with that, Paul?" Mary asked. Bloody hell, I missed that.

"Absolutely, heard every word," I truthfully said.

Mary sighed, kissing me on the forehead gently. "Don't worry, Paul. Get some rest, think you need it. I'll go watch my soaps."

Mary off to her telly and wine, no doubt. Maybe she's right, though—I am bloody knackered. I'll just rest my eyes for a minute, see if that helps. Just a minute or two—that's all. If the pancake let's me, anyway.

Chapter 11 - Just a Little Tumble

Honestly, felt like I'd slept an entire day. Might well have done, even. Bloody hell.

Seems I've a text from the boss man himself. Nice of him to remember I exist.

"Hi Paul, Mark Holland, Securoguard. Can you drop me a call today if you're up for it? TIA."

Bloody Mark. Let me guess—wants me to take a mental health evaluation, or something bloody ridiculous like that. Sod off, Mark, I'm bloody fine, cool and professional just like a cucumber.

Fine, I'll call, have our little chat. I sigh deep, staring off into the ceiling. Am I fine, though? I mean, really?

Either someone drugged me last night, or I'm not dealing with Dick dying as simply as I expected. Which of those seems more logical, more realistic?

Neither, really. Chin up, crack on, that's what Dad always told me. I still miss him, and Mum. I miss Dick too. We weren't best mates, but we saw enough of each other that we were friends. I'll admit to that, even if it is unprofessional.

Dick isn't haunting me. I'm haunting myself.

Enough of that. Phone's out, I'm ready to call Mark. Tap my phone with my finger, staring at the call button. It'll be fine.

"Mark Holland, Sec—"

"Securoguard, yeah, I know. It's Paul, you asked me to Paul."

Bloody hell. Cut him off like a butcher chopping up a pizza. Really need to work on that. Probably.

"Paul? You there?"

"Heard every word Mark, loud and clear. Yeah, I'm fine. So you wanted to talk—couldn't you just have spoken to me at the office when I picked up my keys tonight?"

There was a pause. I can hear his fingers tapping against his desk. Thinking, pondering—scheming?

"You're taking the next two days off, and I've arranged a counsellor for you today."

Gripped my phone tight.

"You're bloody kidding. I'm fine, Mark, I—"

"You can lie to yourself, but not the people who care about you, Paul," he said, cutting me off like a lumberjack felling a tree.

Shook my head, scowling. Bullshit. Care about your income, don't you, Mark. I—I need to listen to this. Professional duty.

"Paul? You there?"

"Sorry, Mark. I'll do it. I'll go."

"Texting you the details, Paul. Keep your chin up, mate. Could be worse."

Click.

Well, that was that I s'pose. Last bloody thing I want is to talk to some poncy therapist, but seems I'll lose my motor if I don't.

Mary?

"Hi, love," she says, appearing in the doorway. Came and sat down next to me, concern painted on her face like a Dickasso.

"Mary, you not cleaning today then, love?" I said, smiling up at her.

"No. Worried about you," she admitted. Bloody hell, am I really worrying people that much? Just a little tumble, that's all. Sodding knees and their mutiny.

"It wasn't just a little tumble, Paul," Mary said.

What the fuck? She heard that? Am I thinking out loud? Is—

Calm down, Paul. Legs feel like bloody jelly and I'm not even stood on them. I miss Dick.

"I'm sure you do," Mary said as she gently rubbed my arm. I missed this. I missed her. I need her.

"I love you so much, Mary," found myself saying. Soppy bloody git. So unprofessional.

"Love you too, Paul. I've a surprise for you downstairs," Mary giggled.

Bloody hell, what's all this then? It my birthday already?

She helps me out of bed—already in my clothes. When did that happen? Off to the kitchen, and... no way. No way!

Roast beef, potatoes with rosemary, peas and carrots and even Yorkshire pudding. Didn't even need my help, cooked the lot herself. Bloody hell, am I dying?

"Just wanted to surprise you, Paul. Look, you scared us all. Think you need to take a few days, and I need to be here for you."

Smell of that meal hit me like a harvester, every bite a sensation old and new. Missed this. Missed her. I should collapse at work more bloody often. Needed to save a Yorkshire pudding though, it could be evidence.

Couldn't eat another bite. I sighed, smiling over at Mary as she smiled right back. Well, time for a little seriousness I s'pose. Keep it professional.

"Mary, I appreciate all this," I began, picking my words carefully like my lottery numbers. Think one was seventeen. "But I'm fine. Just my bloody knees, and—"

"You're not fine, Paul."

I wanted to be mad at being cut off, but I do it too. All the bloody time, in fact. Listen, Paul. Open your ears and listen to the woman you married.

"You called Darren Dick. Multiple times. William, too. Called the paramedic a little green goblin. Darren told us all of this."

75

Bloody hell. That's ridiculous, there's no way I—

But look at her face, Paul. Complicated woman, my wife, but a liar? Nope, never.

"You've been slipping since you found Dick crushed. Not sleeping, glued to your study, reading the same book like a ritual. Thinking out loud, making mistakes—"

"Pancaked," I corrected, cutting her off. Getting too touchy-feely here, love.

Mary sighed. "Not even close. Spoke to Mark. I agree with him—please, see the counsellor. If not for me, or Mark, or Darren, then for yourself, Paul."

Bloody therapist. Why should I—

Stop that train right there, Paul. Look at her. Smile, sure, but look deeper. Pain, fear, love—concern. I need to do this, don't I? Ghosts behind my eyes, legs jelly, head wonky. Sorry, Dad, can't just man my way up out of this one.

"I'll do it. I'll see the therapist."

She gripped my hand, her skin soft in mine. Still those same sparks I felt all those years ago. Ocean felt more like a river today, and I was here for it.

Off we went to my appointment. I felt fine to drive, but Mary insisted. Guess there may be a divide between feeling fine and being fine. Not a particularly professional thought, though.

Doctor's surgery, same old. Clinical, crappy music, notice video with the same information you've seen thousands of times. Chap in the corner with a nasty cough, woman on her phone with a crying baby. And I considered myself a waste of NHS resources.

Checked in, sat down on the plastic chair. The waiting. Monitor flashing up names, but never mine. Mary off sat in the car—she's the smart one. Bloody depressing in here.

Finally. Paul Hope, Room 2, Dr Bartell. Let's go see this therapist then. Surprised they're also a doctor?

Pushed open the door, laminate floor echoing through the hallways as I shuffle through it. Bloody hell, why a woman? I'd find it easier to deal with a man. All business, all professional, none of this touchy-feely rubbish. Waste of everyone's pancakes.

"Hi, Paul, welcome," she said, smiling warmly at me. Long black hair tied back in a ponytail, and dark brown eyes. Interesting-looking lady, this one.

"So I understand you've had a fall at work. Sounds like a dissociative episode from your medical records here."

I speak English, Doc, not bloody French. Je ne comprends pas.

"So, what I mean is, you lost sight of reality for a moment when dealing with trauma. Tell me about your colleague, Dick?"

"Sits between a bloke's legs, Doc. I'm sure you must have seen one or two in your line of work?"

No laugh. Well, I thought it was funny. She just sat typing on her keyboard.

"Well, being married, not as often as I'd like anymore Paul."

Now we're talking! Bloody hell, she got me good with that one. Never saw myself having a good little giggle at a bloody therapy session. Well, guess I best give her what she asked for—Dick. Not mine, obviously, my friend—colleague, rather.

"Colleague. Found the poor bastard pancaked by a harvester on patrol."

More tapping away on those keys. What's she writing, then? Some kind of commendation I expect.

"You'll forgive me if I don't ask you for the recipe then, Paul."

Recipe? What is—oh—oh! Bloody pancakes! Bloody hell, she should come to improv. She'd be a sodding natural. Christ, more of this and my lungs will start to hurt.

"How'd it feel when you found him?"

77

That was a more therapist-y thing to say. Fun's over, I guess. No daft, no silly, just... this.

"Scared," I admitted. Felt it slip without thinking about it. Weird, that.

"Scared how?" she pressed. Let it go, love, that was enough for me. I'm fine, really.

"Could happen to him, could happen to me."

Sandra nodded. Wait, is her name Sandra?

"Sandra."

Bloody hell. Don't tell me I thought out loud again. Get it together, Dick.

Paul. Bloody Paul. Christ.

More tippy-tapping away on those keys of hers. I must be impressing her.

"I can understand how that must make you feel scared. You saw a man crushed by a harvester—you found him."

I narrowed my gaze. Hold on a bloody minute—when had I told her about that?

"Just a moment ago," Sandra said. No, Sandra. Dick, mate, get out from under my eyelids a minute and just let me talk here. This feels important.

"Yeah," I began. "Just... a pancake. Lifeless face, gazing off into the abyss, body flat under the... timing. The timing, too."

Yeah. That did feel a little—a bit odd. Pizzas and pancakes. Pizzas one night and pancakes the next.

More tapping. "His death was ruled an accident? Did it look like one to you?"

What the hell kind of stupid bloody question is that? Do I look like a bloody detective to you, Dick?

"Sandra."

Fuck. Sorry.

I sighed deep, trying to bat Dick away from under my eyelids. When is the last time I slept properly without being haunted? Why wouldn't he just let me focus, and rest?

"I'm scared," I slipped.

"It's understandable, Dick. You saw Dick get crushed under a piece of farm machinery, and you barely missed a beat. Threw yourself straight back into work and shrugged it off, calling it a pancake."

I couldn't help but chuckle. Not about the Dick pancake thing, or her calling me Dick, no. That's probably the longest sentence I've sat and listened to in a long bloody time.

I wanted to argue. I wanted to say I'm fine, I've a shift starting in three hours, I have to go. But I couldn't. I didn't. Seems I'd joined my bloody knees in the mutiny.

"Let's start by giving you some medication, Paul. Something to help you sleep, something to help with the anxiety."

Anxiety? Pish. I'm fine.

"I need to work," I said. "I've got to keep busy."

"I'm signing you off this week, and we're not arguing about that."

Bloody hell. Can tell she's married. Still, have to respect a straight edge. I'll try your bloody pills, Doc.

"I'll teach you a technique to help you stay focused at work—it's called grounding."

Therapist mumbo-jumbo. But I'll listen.

"Think of it like a tool. If you feel yourself getting overwhelmed, ground yourself in your senses. Name something you can see, feel, hear, smell and taste. Repeat it two or three times, if necessary. Does that make sense?"

Hmm. Kind of does, actually. I don't hate the idea—just a tool, that's all.

"Thanks, Sandra. I'm still scared," I slipped again, mouth like a bloody sieve. Can I stop saying that already? Bloody ridiculous. Pancakes and pizza.

"You've been through something traumatic, Paul. Let yourself feel your feelings, whatever those may be. I want us to book regular Friday afternoon therapy sessions moving forwards—at least until you feel better."

"I feel fine now, Doc," I said. Getting a bit too emotional here, feels very unprofessional. Need to nip this in the pancake.

"Do you?" she asked simply.

Do I? That's the million-quid question I s'pose, isn't it. I tell myself I'm fine, always have. But thinking fine is feeling fine, isn't it? Chin up, like Dad always said.

"I don't honestly know," I admitted. "Feels complicated."

"Trauma often is. I'll see you next week, Paul. Take care, take rest."

Just like that, got my pills, back in the car, Mary driving me home. Yet somehow, things feel different—more complicated than they were before.

Mary sat with me in the living room. No wine, no soaps, just next to each other on the sofa, her hand in mine like we used to.

Ocean's still there, I know. I'm not fooling myself here. But things feel... different. Less stormy? Probably.

"Paul, got something to tell you," Mary said.

Oh dear. Hurricane? Tornado? Inter-galactic sentient cheesecake?

"Paul, when I found that weed at the school. Before the boy left, I mean. Do you remember?"

I do. Why's she bringing that up now? Didn't we sort that out? Pizza and pancakes.

I simply nodded. She wasn't looking at me. Her lips smiled but her eyes didn't. Mary?

"Paul, I saw a teacher there. I'm sure of it. I think there was more, and in his panic, he left the one I found."

She audibly sighed, releasing that tension. How long had she been holding that in? And why?

"Didn't feel I could share, Paul. I was worried."

Telly. Lavender. Ticking clock. Mary's skin, soft against mine, as we held hands.

"Did you see the teacher? Was it Stephen, tired-looking one with glasses from improv?" I asked, mind wandering back to his panic attack at improv.

"I only came twice, but I don't think so, no. I only saw him for a second as he rushed off, love, but he seemed taller, broader. You've been complaining about kids and bloody stoners, Paul, but I think—"

"Pizza and pancakes," I remarked, cutting Mary off.

"Paul, listen. Something feels off. Don't you see it? Don't you agree?"

Too many true crime documentaries and police procedurals, Mary. When you're not with your soaps, that is. I feel like your bit on the side next to those sometimes.

"That's fair. I do get wrapped up in them, I admit. I'm sorry, Paul."

Bollocks. Telly, clock, cheesecake—

"I'm sorry too, Mary. I'm no better, with my books. Sunday, our day, like we used to. What do you say?"

She smiled. It reached her eyes. "I'd like that, Paul. But please, be careful. This doesn't feel like teenage pot smoking, love. Not like we used to," Mary mused.

Ahh. To be young and dumb again. To be a bloody stoner. Functional knees that weren't actively trying to mutiny might help too.

Her words stuck. I heard them. Be careful. Pizza and pancakes.

Chapter 12 - Bloody Aliens

Dick beneath my eyes again. But this time, wasn't haunting me. Was just... there. I'm on it, Dick. I heard you.

Should thank him for finally letting me get a little rest, really. I'm too bloody old for these sleepless nights.

Also too bloody old to be wrapped up in all this drama. So bloody unprofessional. Pizza and pancakes.

Still, Friday eve now. Dreading the next one—I'll have to speak to Sandra first. Bloody therapy.

Still, she was absolutely hilarious. Could actually see her enjoying improv club. Wouldn't be unprofessional either, would it? Not like I'm inviting her to dinner. It's a public club—anyone is welcome. Even a grumpy old git like me.

Pull into car park, community centre. Hannah here, nice and early. Stephen too? He's been coming early past couple of weeks. Wonder if they're canoodling. I like the idea of that, somehow. They're both bloody lonely, that much is obvious.

"Hi, Paul!" Hannah beamed, seeing me approach. Bloody hell, her energy is infectious. No wonder she sells so many of those star witnesses.

"Hah! Star witness! I see that harvester joke stuck, Paul," she giggled with a smile.

Bloody hell. Taste coffee, smell cheap floor polish, see Stephen with his bloodshot eyes and... bloody hell, when's the last time he even slept?

He smiled at seeing me, but it daren't reach his bloodshot eyes. Poor bugger looks like Atlas, weight on his shoulders. Must talk to him later. Pizzas and pancakes.

"Hungry, Paul?" Hannah asked, that trademark smile on her face.

"Bloody am, actually. Going to eat a few of your chocolate digestives," I reply. God bless her for bringing these biscuits with. A cranky old git suggested it a few months back, and she loved the idea. Doesn't even charge us for them. Need more kindness like hers in the world, I'm sure.

Too touchy-feely again though. Bloody hell. Well, the others are pouring in—including that brooding detective Tom. Swear he's just here to laugh at us, I never see him join in.

"Paul, come sit a moment," Hannah said gently. "Been worried about you. Mark said you had a fall, took some time off?"

Bloody hell. I'm not going through this again.

"Yeah. I'm fine though, just tired. You know Mark?"

Hannah sat beside me, arm round my shoulder. "I do, from the farm. Small community, we all know each other, silly!"

Right. Makes sense. Barely a handful of us living here. One less, now, with Dick a pancake.

"It's perfectly alright not to be fine," Hannah suggested. But I am fine. Fine as dandy. What even is dandy, anyway? Maybe it should be shandy. Could go for one of those right now.

"I see his face," I slipped. "Staring into the abyss. Lifeless."

"Aww. Poor thing," Hannah said, squeezing my shoulder. "Come on. Let's get you up, get you playing, put that behind you."

Right. Seems we're up and ready now. Zip zap cheesecake and we're ready to go. Not sure I'm feeling this tonight, though, if I'm really honest with myself. Might just sit back and watch a bit.

"Need some volunteers!" Hannah announced. "How about our newcomer?"

"Love to!" Dick said, rushing from his seat.

Darren. Bloody Darren, not Dick. Hold on—Darren is here?

Right. I invited him. I think. No, I did. Definitely. Probably.

Floor polish, biscuit, buzzing light.

"How about you then, Stephen?" Hannah gently suggested. Could see him and Di—Darren working well together.

"Not feeling it," Stephen mumbled. Bloody miseryguts.

"Paul?"

I don't feel it either really. But the mood in here, it's a bloody morgue. Better hop in, cheer these misers up, really.

"Love to, what's my prompt then, love?" I say, groaning from my stupid bloody wonky chair. How'd I get lumbered with this bloody rubbish when I weren't last here?

"Darren, was it? You're an alien trying to blend in with humans. Paul, you're a Dick pancake. Go!"

I'm a bloody what?

"Come again?" I ask. "What am I?"

"Alien also trying to be human!" Hannah whispered. Right. Let's do it.

"Ahem... so eating things, am I right, fellow human?" I said.

Darren already grinning, coming up with ideas. Can hear those cogs turning.

"Why yes, fellow human with a complex digestive system and a need for oxygen! What brings you to this fine planet?"

Bloody hell! Planet? He's onto me. Must know I'm an alien.

Giggles from the crowd. Let's think.

85

"I heard about those cheesecakes you humans—we humans, rather, like to eat! I brought one with me from the planet Zipzazzagar."

More chuckles.

"Bloody hell," Darren said. "Don't think you can get much more human than that, can you, Paul?"

"Lovely, lovely, you two," Hannah said. "Come on then, let's have Stephen and Tom?"

"Fine watching," Tom muttered. Bloody hell, mate, play along, won't you.

Stephen busy chewing his nails like it's an Olympic sport. He met eyes with Hannah then darted out the room. He's not very bloody professional for a teacher.

"Guess not. You mind checking on him, Paul?" Hannah asked. "Come on, Darren, play with me."

"Yes, dear," Dick said, already stood from our session a moment ago.

Right then. I'll go see what the teacher is crying about. Shuffled out the room, and—right, can't bloody forget. Need to talk to him anyway, about pizzas and pancakes.

"Stephen?" I said gently, seeing him sat on a bench outside, folded up like a lawn chair. Hunched up, rather. Either I s'pose.

"What do you want, Paul," he muttered back, deflated. Bloody hell, just trying to cheer the poor bugger up here.

"Don't need cheering up," he muttered more, but his face betrayed his words like a harvester betrayed a pancake. He did. He really bloody did.

"Wait!" I announced. Mary, lockers, teachers, pizzas. "Listen, Stephen."

Took a deep breath. Counted to three. Exhaled.

"Bloody teacher dealing weed at your posh git school."

Stephen snapped to attention like a mousetrap, turning to me as the colour drained from his face.

"What? What do you mean? What teacher? What happened?"

"Bloody hell, Stephen, one question at a time, mate. Right, let me focus here, I need to tell him. Tell you, I mean."

Rambling, Paul. Back on the track, focus. Pizzas and pancakes.

"My wife cleans there, time to time. Caught a teacher going for that weed behind the lockers."

Bloody hell, calm down, Stephen. You'll run out of nails to chew.

"She see him? Who is it? What did he look like? Did she talk to the police? Did you?"

"Dick, mate, calm down," I began. "None of—"

"Who's Dick?" he said, cutting me off like a knife through a lemon cheesecake.

"Sorry, Gary. Still dealing with his death. Got pancaked by a harvester on duty."

His face white as a sheet now, visibly shaking. Bloody hell, Stephen, get it together. Just a little pancake.

"A har—har—harvester? Flattened him?" he stuttered like a stuck record.

"Right. Well, thought you might need to know about the teacher with the weed, Stephen. Not just a bloody stoner after all, is it?"

Looked like he tried to hunch himself up into a ball by this point. Bloody hell, what's his problem?

"This is serious, Paul," he said. "Did your wife see the teacher? Did you tell anyone?"

"Already told you no, mate. Clear your bloody ears out!" I jabbed with a chuckle. He was in no laughing mood, looked like he was about to cry. Bugger.

"I need to go. I need to think. I need—"

"Dick, mate, you alright? You're panick—"

"Fine! I'm fine. I just need to go. Need to think. Don't say anything, Paul. Let me dig. Let me look. Let me—"

"Stephen, calm down," I said. He was sweating, shaking, breathing heavy. Bloody hell. Just a bit of weed, mate.

No. It wasn't though, was it? Pizzas and pancakes. Watched Stephen dash off, hop in his car, go. Bloody hell, he didn't take that very well, did he? Was that—what was that?

Think, Paul. Bloody think. That was no normal reaction, was it? That was panic. Fear... guilt? Can't be. No, can't be. Mary said it wasn't—

But she only saw him twice, didn't she? They weren't exactly known to each other. Could she be mistaken? Could I have just told the bloody dealer that he's bloody dealing? Bloody hell! What do I bloody do?

Calm down, sodding samba in my ears. Knackered old heart—don't you bloody mutiny as well. Do I talk to Stephen again? Find out what he knows? Do I talk to Tom? He's a bloody detective. To Mary again? Have I put her in danger?

Christ, Paul. What have you gotten yourself involved in, here? Pizzas and bloody pancakes.

Chapter 13 - Pizza plus Pancakes

Bloody hell! Breathe, Paul. Breathe.

Hands on steering wheel, strangling the leather. Tyres humming in my ears. Lights from other drivers, dazzling my bloody eyes. Bloody hell, what else was it? Fiddlesticks!

I'm clearly not myself. Doesn't take a therapist to see that, does it. So bloody unprofessional of me.

At the same time, no mistaking that reaction from Stephen. Might as well have been a bloody intergalactic cheesecake up in the sky—Stephen's bloody involved in the pizzas and pancakes. Can't doubt that.

I saw his reaction. Sweating like a pig, panic like a disco, his face a bloody manuscript written with guilt and spaghetti.

Leather wheel, tyre hum, bright lights, metal in my throat. Christ, need some water.

Pull into the driveway, race inside practically bursting through the door. Mary. Where's Mary?

Armchair, bottle of wine, sleeping like a tiger. Bless her. Need to calm these racing thoughts, just take a deep breath. Focus, be professional.

Do I tell her? Instincts tell me to keep her out of this. Don't want her in danger, or getting emotional.

But I need to accept the fact that my instincts have been a bit bloody wonky lately. I saw Dick get crushed by a—bloody pancake. Pizzas and pancakes.

Focus, Paul. Mary. I have to keep this from her, but—

I gently tapped Mary on the shoulder. Just going to see how she is. Not telling her.

"Paul? You OK, love?" she mumbled like a tiger, stirring from her slumber.

"Pizzas and pancakes," I blurted out. Why'd you go and say that for, Paul.

"Paul?"

"Sorry, love. It's nothi—no. No it isn't."

STOP! You could be putting her in danger. No, idiot—you already bloody have by telling sodding dealie-McStevie, you old nitwit. Bloody talk to your wife already. Sit.

Took a seat across from Mary. I can hear the telly, smell the wine, see my beautiful wife still gorgeous despite the weathers of time. Bit bloody unprofessional that but it's true. Her eyes still sparkling like diamonds atop the cheesecake in the sky.

"Paul?"

Oh. Right. Conversation. Conversation about pizzas and pancakes. Focus, Paul.

"We've not stumbled onto teenage stoners dealing weed here, Mary," I began. Stop now, that's enough, can't— "I told Stephen what you saw. The way he reacted, Mary, I—are you sure it wasn't him?"

Enough. Enough already. Stop. Unprofessional, isn't it.

"Honestly, Paul, no. I'm not sure it wasn't him. I've only seen the man twice, and I barely caught a glimpse of him at the lockers. It... could have been."

Could have been. Possibility plus plausibility plus pizza plus pancakes. We're onto something here.

But my head is fuzzy like a peach playing piano. I sigh, hands on my aching knees, Mary's smile warm to the touch. I—I need to take my pills and get some bloody rest.

Real rest, not the Dick eyelid sleepless nights I've been having. And... that bloody Sandra. My therapist. I need to see her, too.

"You're right, Paul. I'm so glad to hear you say that."

Blurting my bloody thoughts out again. Need to work on that.

Shook my head, stilled my thoughts. I've a plan, and it's going to work.

Analogue clock in the kitchen. I haven't changed the bloody battery in years. Thing always pissed me off, tick tock, calming, grounding.

Well, I need it now. Getting that done, sorting it. First, I need to talk to Mary, address the cheesecake in the room.

"Mary, I'm worried about these drugs. Have I put you in danger by telling Stephen?"

Studied her expression, best I could. She knew something, I could tell. What did she know? Who?

"I can't really see why, Paul. Just a cleaner, me."

Said with such precision, such practice, so skilfully said like a tiger singing—what do tigers sing anyway? I sighed deep. Head, calm. Tick, tock.

"Your words betray you, my love," I blurted. "I hear the concern. I'm sorry."

Bloody unprofessional, that.

"It's not your fault, Paul. I shouldn't have tried to put your mind at ease—we have a communication problem. Let's get you well again, rest, medicine, therapy."

She sighed deep before continuing.

"Then let's... let's bloody look into these dealing bastards, Paul. Children, Paul. Dealing at a posh private school. I can't sit idly by—can you?"

Don't suppose I bloody can either. Hugely unprofessional, dealing to kids. Little smiling faces, eating their slices of pizza, weed stuffed in bags behind the lockers. No, this has to stop. Pizzas and pancakes.

Pancakes. Dick.

Harvester. Star witness.

"Bloody hell, Mary," I said, yawning, "was the bloody—is the harvester pancake part of—did the—"

"Calm down, Paul. What are you trying to tell me?"

91

I am bloody calm. Never been calmer. Cool, cold, professional as ever.

"Scared. I'm scared they killed Dick. The timing of the accident was—was bloody uncanny, weren't it?"

Oops! That slipped out. Come back here, words.

Too late. Can see Mary frowning now. She's giving my crazy old crackpot gibberish some pause. Write it off, Mary, I'm just going barmy here.

"No, you might have a point. But how the hell would you even go about proving something like that?"

Bloody impossible, I think. Only people I know who know anything about harvesters and farm machinery are the farmer chap who owns the farm, Hannah, and Mark. Maybe Claire too? She used to be a horse. No, worked with horses. That made less sense.

Mark bloody Holland is the son of a big farmer. Potatoes, I think? Might have been potatoes actually. What was that bloody farmer's name anyway? Wasn't it George? I'll ask Dick. He'll know.

Wait. Bloody can't, can I, harvester made him into a pancake. But what was the harvester called?

"Paul, I want you to get some rest. Mark called me, concerned about you. You're to take the month off."

Month off? Not professional. I need to nip this in the bud, get back to my work.

"Yes, dear. I need the rest."

Bloody mouth running away from me again. Had enough of these sodding mutinies.

But she's right. Rest, medicine, therapy.

Rest, medicine, therapy.

First on the list? Rest.

Chapter 14 - Bloody Mechanics

Two weeks passed me by. No improv last week—community centre hired out for a bloody wedding. Thought Hannah had it booked up all year, but I guess not.

Been seeing my therapist more often. Off to see her right now, in fact, pulling into the car park. Bloody doctors.

Taking the bucket of pills she gave me, too, when they allow it. Can't read half the bloody labels—eyes are fine, just weird jumbly moxycyliwhateveracin. No idea, do as I'm told me. Cool as a cucumber.

Well, here we go. Assuming my bloody knees let me, anyway. Seem a bit more cooperative these days, since the pills. No more falls, thank God.

Waiting room. Cheap plastic chair, uncomfortable. Even cheaper disinfectant, stinks. Bright buzzing lights. Nice and cool.

Buzzing me in already. Grin as I walk past these poor sods still sat here waiting. Almost made me feel like a VIP.

"Welcome, Paul. How are we feeling?" Sandra said, as I clicked the door shut behind me.

"Fan-bloody-tastic," I proclaimed. "Sharper, clearer, better."

Sandra shook her head. "Functional. But you're still dealing with a lot, Paul, including grief over the—"

"I'm fine, really," cutting her off like scissors through ribbon. Damn, been trying to work on that.

"Sorry," I offer meekly.

Warm smile lit up her face like a Christmas tree. Wonder what I'd said to prompt that? Thinking about cheesecake maybe. I haven't had one myself in years.

"You're making fine progress, Paul. Still off the road for the next two weeks, then?"

"Yes, that's right. Bit unprofessional, but boss mandated some rest. Both bosses, actually," I chuckle, fiddling with my wedding ring.

"Still hiding your feelings behind that faux professionalism too, I see?"

I laughed out loud. "Hey, nothing faux about it. I'm all business, edge of a razor, claw of a crab me."

"Crabs have pincers," Sandra corrected with a smirk.

"Same thing."

Got her laughing with that one. I'm the first to admit it, I do have an active imagination. I get inspired by all those stars on my night rounds.

"Well, you've been keeping up with your pills, your therapy, your grounding techniques?"

"All of 'em, Sandra. My mantra, too—helps me focus on my work concerns."

"Oh?"

Ah bloody hell. There goes my mouth again, running like a doe from a lion. Or was it a tiger? Can't remember. Guess I better explain.

"Pizzas and pancakes. Keeps me focused on the...issues."

Sandra narrowed her gaze. Felt her looking right through me. Bloody hell.

"What's got you scared, Paul?" she asked.

"I don't get scared. Unprofessional—"

"Paul."

Bloody hell. Makes me feel like I'm a toddler back in playgroup sometimes. Fine, fine.

"Harvester accident. My head nice and clear, it... it really feels less like an accident, Sandra."

Tapping away at her keyboard. What's she typing there then?

"I looked it up after our last talk. Police investigated it, found no evidence of wrongdoing. Do you feel you may be projecting, Paul?"

She paused a moment, leaning in closer.

"Look. Sudden, accidental death is... difficult. Takes your breath away. Trying to attribute meaning to it may be your way of coping."

Sighed, clenching my fists. No. I'm not a barmy old man here. OK, I'm exactly that, but I'm onto something.

"Timing was off," I said. "He warned me about cannabis dealers the night before."

"And what would it mean if it was an accident? Just random, meaningless, no conspiracies or controversies?"

Bollocks. Bit direct, Sandra, but really making me think here. Am I chasing ghosts? Am I trying to give Dick's death a meaning beyond a random bloody harvester accident?

"No, not very professional that. It has to mean something."

"Does it? Or does grief want to make sense of senselessness?"

Bloody hell. So many questions, and they're all bloody thoughtful. Really though, what's more likely—that he was murdered over a bit of weed, or nobody bothered fixing up that harvester for yonks? Bloody mechanics. I was still trying to remember his name, but it wasn't coming to me.

"Paul?"

"Appreciate your counsel, Sandra. You really do give a shit, you know that? Say, you consider my offer for Friday night improv?"

Offered me a warm smile. Not her thing, I guess. Or maybe professional boundaries? Who knew.

"Not sure it's appropriate, Paul. See you next week. Let's dial down the sessions to every Friday again, alright? You're doing great."

Doing great, feeling fine. Fine as shandy. Star witness popped into my head with a cruel smile. Bloody harvester.

"Thanks. Next week then," I said before hopping on out of there. Not literally, of course—bloody knees would never allow it.

Right then. Get home, spend some time with Mary. We've taken to using my study for our little project now. We're taking photographs, writing down ideas and connections. Proper little mystery club, Sherlock and Watson. But which one am I?

Gripped my wheel tight, pulling into the driveway. Let's go see what we've got—Mary's been bloody busy whilst I've been getting better.

"Hey, love," Mary said from the study, rushing up to come give me a hug. Soft and warm, just like a tiger.

"Mary. Thought I'd come look at our little project again. Where we at this time?"

"You're going to love this, Paul," Mary began.

I'm already on the edge of my seat.

"Spill the soup already, love," I said.

"Oh right! So I left my phone recording video, tucked it away at the lockers when I figured Stephen would be there. I didn't catch him, I'm sorry."

Bugger.

"But."

But! But! Buttered bread! But what?

"I caught bloody Brian."

"No sodding way! Brian, the static cover guard? He's moved a lot, providing absence cover for pretty much all of Mark's sites—same as Claire!"

"Jesus," Mary muttered, writing that down. "That gives them access to, well..."

"Bloody everything!" I finish.

"Yeah."

Pulled out her phone. Little bag, but still him. Undeniable video evidence that this rambling old man isn't crazy. Pizzas and pancakes. It's not enough—but it's a bloody good start. Very professional, my wife.

"That's video evidence of handling cannabis, Paul. Do we go to the police?"

Books. Wooden desk beneath my hand. Pen I'm chewing. Delicious.

"You look tired, Paul. Do we take a break?"

"No to both, love. Too soon for police. Barely a baggie in the video—they'll laugh us out the station. But I know a detective? Sort of."

Bloody Tom. Stoic Tom. Tom the sodding miser who sits and watches improv but barely bloody joins in.

"We could consider asking him—unless you feel we need more first?"

Getting tired. Just need a minute. Shuffle off, afternoon pills, cup of tea. Back I go, tea for Mary too. I'm professional like that.

Right then, let's have a look at the table. I've called it Project Pizzas and Pancakes. Or maybe it should be Operation instead of Project? No bloody idea.

We've got Jake. He drives pizzas. Another unknown pizza delivery driver. Brian—he's involved, Mary just confirmed it. Stephen likely is too, but he's being bloody shifty now.

"Think we should go over the harvester again, love," I say to Mary. "Star witness."

Set down her pen, met my eyes.

"I have my doubts, Paul. But if you're right about this..."

"Then it was deliberate. It was no accident, it was... it was... pancake."

"No, Paul. Murder."

Bloody hell! Bookshelf, delicious plastic pen, carpet under my feet, birds chirping outside—

The words were heavy, hanging in the air like an anchor. I wanted to dream of aliens and sentient spatulas and interdimensional cheesecakes just to run from it. But I couldn't.

Murder.

Tapped my delicious pen against the desk, staring at the notebooks scattered atop it. Grabbed a new one and wrote "Pancake".

Operation Pizzas and Pancakes. Let's commit to this, document what we know.

"So, who had access to that site?"

"Bloody farmer, and any site visitors he had that day. But it's bloody busy, no real way someone could have set that up in the daytime."

Ran my hand through my stubble, sat across my study desk from Mary. Caught myself gazing at her quite a while.

"What?" she said, catching me stare.

"Nothing. You're just gorgeous," I slipped. Not very professional that, but I was no liar.

"Been too long since you looked at me like that, Paul," she said with a smile, reaching her eyes.

"I'm here now, Mary. Not like that bloody cheesecake I keep forgetting to buy."

That got her chuckling. All that heavy stuff on the desk, but sat across it we were still husband and wife, Paul and Mary.

"Come on, you. It's been forever, and this is bloody happening," she said with a wicked grin.

Up she got. Right, off to the bedroom then. Pizzas and pancakes can wait till morning.

Chapter 15 - Happy bloody Lorry

Another therapy session behind me. Doing the work, feeling fine as shandy, nice and professional. Hopefully I can go back to my motor soon.

Been hard at work with Mary in the study. Things aren't perfect, we still have our moments—but actually starting to feel like a team again. She's so bloody professional.

Bloody hell. Call from Mark. Best answer.

"Hi, Paul, Mark Holland, Securo—"

Yeah, yeah. Securobloodyguard Services, bloody know already, mate. Crack on with it. Honestly doesn't need to say that every time, does he? Almost makes it seem less professional. Muppet.

"So what do you think?" Mark said.

Bloody hell. Missed the lot. Zoned out like a sleepy cat.

"Sorry, Mark. I heard most of it but not all, mate. Can you run that by me again?"

"Oddly honest for you, Paul. Can tell you've been talking to a therapist, mate—happy to see it. I want you to be my trainer for the next two weeks, Paul."

Trainer? Bloody trainer? Teaching new hires? Bloody hell. Can't think of anything worse. Not bloody professional.

"I'll do it," I announced quickly, though I couldn't fathom bloody why. Mouth running like a fridge again.

"Great! I've a new starter next week for you. And Brian will be learning mobile duties too."

Brian? Bloody Brian with the wacky baccy? Does Mark know? How bloody could he? They're taking him for a fool. Do I tell him?

Hold on, though. If I'm training up Brian, I can watch him. See how bloody professional he really is now, can't I?

Coffee cup. Musty books. Tasty pen.

"You there, Paul?"

"Sorry, Mark, the cogs in the old noggin whirring away. Yes, I'll do it. Let me know when and where," I announced.

"Great. Rest up and feel better meanwhile. Take care, Paul," he said before hanging up like the washing.

Well, that'll help me feel better I s'pose. Not sure I want to train people, but somehow my motor mouth mugged me into it. Bloody thing. Runs away from me like fatherhood did.

Besides, keep an eye on Brian. Need to know what's going on here, don't we. Pizzas and pancakes.

Still. Improv back on tonight. Not exactly a smoking gun, video Mary got, and it was filmed without consent. Clearly see Brian messing with a bag of weed, though.

Could be enough to get Tom's attention. That or he might laugh me out the community centre, who knows.

Nervous. First proper social event since I had my tiny little tumble. Or was it? Can't remember. Stay cool, Paul. Just like the cucumber.

Really need to look that up later. Keeps popping in my head and I've no idea what it bloody means. Probably something off the telly—usually is.

I've pulled into the community centre now. Right— Stephen's car is here, and he's getting collared after. Maybe before, seeing him approach my car. What's all this then?

Tapped on my window. Look like he hasn't slept in two bloody weeks, poor bastard. Be professional, Paul.

Window down, he leans in close. Stinks of bloody beer. Or is that vodka? Awful, either way.

"Paul," he slurred, "am shorry. I overreacted."

"Bloody hell are you on about, mate?" I asked, cool and professional like the proverbial cucumber. "You dealing to fucking kids? Fuck is wrong with—"

"PAUL!" he yells, droplets of beer spit spluttering out his gob. "Keep your voish down. It's not like—hic—it's"

"Hey, guys!" Hannah says, wandering over. Startled Stephen so much he bloody falls on the floor! Laughing my eyes out here. Or maybe he's just that drunk? Who knows.

"Stephen? You alright?" Hannah says, rushing over to him.

"Fine! Fine. Get off," he mumbles as she tries to help him up. Not very bloody professional, is it, Stephen. Disappointing, that.

Hannah makes a face at him, getting me giggling. He deserved it, that was very unkind. Or maybe unprofessional. Not sure.

"Go home and rest, Stephen," Hannah says gently.

He shuffled off towards his car. Wait—did he bloody drive here in that state? Bloody hell!

Rush out my seat, run over, grab his damn keys as he's trying to jam them into his car door. Not bloody happening, mate.

Cold keys. Hannah's concerned frown. Stephen's stinky booze breath. Calm like the cheesecake.

"Right. I'm driving this muppet home," I said, nice and cool, calm. Bloody pancakes.

"Sure thing, Paul, thank you. See to it that he's OK. You doing any better yourself?" Hannah asked, smile warming me like a toaster in the bathtu—

Bit too warm that actually. Like a kettle? Kettles are warm.

"Paul?"

"Sorry, Hannah, off with the aliens again," I remark. "I'm fine as shandy, me. I'll get him home, then come back and play!" I announce happily.

Nice to see that put a smile back on her face. Stephen clearly worried her. Idiot.

Right then. Get this drunk muppet into my motor and drive him home. If he's sober enough to tell me where that is, anyway.

"Stephen, you silly sausage," I say, wondering how sausages are silly in the first place, "where do you bloody live, mate?"

"Not going home!" he slurs. "More drink!"

Know what? I'll take him to the pub for a pint. Get him talking, nice bit of professional evidence gathering. He's drunk, so he'll be nice and loose too.

"I'm worried you've had enough already, Stephen," I state. "But I'll take you Bear's Paw for some coff—"

"NO!" he yells, cutting me off like a scalpel. "Anywhere but—hic—there."

Well. That was bloody interesting, wasn't it? Why's he so scared of the Paw? Just another pub, ain't it. Nothing special.

"Right, well, you can't stay here and you don't want to go ho—"

"Happy Meal," he cuts me off again like a drunk nitwit. "Get me a Happy Meal."

"Those are for bloody kids, mate. Like the ones you deal to, you tosser," I state nice and cool. Professional.

"Just... take me. We'll talk."

Fine. I'll drive this bugger to the bloody bright arches and get him his kids meal. See what he's got to say for himself.

Right then. Grip my wheel tight, as he splutters next to me. Had to strap him in like a bloody child. Bloody idiot.

"Happy Meal please," I say, pulling up next to the speaker.

"Welcome to McDonald's, take you order please?" the young bored-sounding lady said.

Oh right. I need them to talk to me first or they don't hear me. Or is she ignoring me? Or just—

Stay professional here, Paul. Drunk lout next to me has me on edge. I recognise that. Right, well—

"Hello?"

"Sorry, sorry. I'll take a Happy Meal please."

"Which one?"

"The bloody happy one? What do you mean which bloody one?"

"Sir, no need to be rude. You can choose fish fingers, cheesebur—"

Rude? What bloody rude? Soft these kids. I'm all bloody professional. Damn, I missed the choices. Looks like you're getting fish fingers, Stephen.

"Fish fingers."

"Drink?"

Bloody hell, what is this? Twenty questions? Who wants to be a Millionaire? Christ.

"Drink."

"Right, which drink?"

"Cola."

"Diet or regular?"

Grip my wheel so tight my knuckles turn white. About to pop a bloody gasket here.

"Regular."

"Great, pull up to the—"

I drive off to the next window. Not listening to all that bloody nonsense.

Feel the wheel. Stephen still stinks. See this strangely familiar young lady, but don't know who she is.

"Sorry. Here," tap the plastic as she glares at me. Who ruffled her flowers then?

Drive to the next window, get this big muppet his kids meal. Nice and fast, efficient, professional. Take him to a nearby car park, pull into a dark corner. Trees hang overhead, quiet around. Darkness has fallen.

"Here's your bloody happy meal. Drink the cola, it'll help sober you up, you tosser," I say, all business, polite and cool, like the cucumber.

Time passes. Munches on his fish fingers, slurps the Coke. He ain't sober, but he's not quite so... unprofessional.

"Paul," he mumbles finally. "Can't go to the Paw. They're there."

"Who?"

"They—I'm compromised," Stephen slurs.

Compromised? What does that bloody mean? Bloody pizzas and pancakes.

"No more cryptic bollocks," I say, nice and cool. "You deal to kids, you evil arsehole. Now why?"

"They made me!" he blurts, sobbing, crying like a toddler who just dropped their slice of cheesecake.

Bloody hell. All this crying, this blubbering mess of emotions, not bloody professional, is it. Might need to buy him another Happy Meal, this one isn't working.

"Talk to me, Stephen. What's happening? What have you got yourself into, you nitwit?"

Still sat sobbing. Christ.

"Blackmail. They have... they have—hic—hictures."

"Pictures?"

"Pictures! I'm fucking naked, Paul!"

Bloody hell, roaring like a waterfall on steroids now. Watch him go. What's he trying to tell me here? He isn't naked. Wearing his same bloody—

Wait. Blackmail. Pictures. Pizza and pancakes.

Bloody hell. He's no sodding dealer. Bloody idiot is a victim.

Need to change tactics here. Get him talking. Cool and cucumber.

"Gary," I say, soft as frozen butter, "I'm sorry. I didn't mean to be so harsh. What bloody happened?"

"Are you calling the police?" he mumbled. Seemed a touch less plastered now, but still not sober as a shrimp.

"Not ringing the old bill, mate, but you need to talk," I gently suggested.

"Started online, I—"

Uh-oh. He's retching. Quickly lowered his window so he can chuck up out the window. Bloody hell, thank god I got the window down in time, right bloody mess. Bloody happy meal.

"Better?" I ask, not a hint of sarcasm. Probably.

"Fuck you, Paul," he stated plainly. Seeming a lot better now.

"Married man, mate. Besides, you ain't my type," I state professionally. Bloody teacher.

Glare at the bastard. He doesn't want to talk, but he's going to. I'm like a headache that just won't go away.

"Talk." I demand.

Bit sharp for me, but I deserved answers.

"Dating app. I was, I got divorced. Year ago," he began. "I met this woman online, and she seemed so—"

Christ, does his breath stink. Mouth's a bloody brewery. And what's this bloody romance novel he's spewing about anyway? Bloody boring—bugger, need to pay attention.

"And... well... all I have to do is make sure the packages are picked up and given to the right people."

"Bloody hell," I say, "I missed all that. Can you repeat the part about the um, the bloody, the uh"

"Dating app?"

"Yeah, yeah, that's it. I'm listening," I lied. Bloody hell. Steering wheel, Stephen's ugly mug, his bloody brewery breath—

"—She got me fully naked after that. Used it as leverage ever since. If it gets out, I'm finished, Paul. Lose my job—lose everything."

Caught enough of that. Gave scammer a picture of his dingle dangle, she's blackmailed him. Wonder why it's called that anyway? Bet Mary would know. She's bloody smart. Still, no idea why his email was important, but I was listening. Probably.

"Paul?"

"So stop helping them then," I abruptly announced. "You're putting kids in danger here."

"I know! I bloody know, Paul! You think I don't? I—I never wanted this, I—"

"So you chose your own hide over the bloody kids then? That it? You fucked up and instead of owning up to it, you let kids get hooked on weed. Scum," I say, nice and professional.

Actually, no, I think I was a bit harsh. He's crying again. Bloody hell.

"Sorry, Stephen, didn't—"

"No but you're bloody right, aren't you, Paul?" he sobbed. "No word a lie. No word."

Bloody hell. Maybe I should go buy him another kids meal. Wonder if they do ones with cheesecake? Keep bloody forgetting to buy that.

"Pizza and pancakes," I blurt out.

"Huh?" he grunts, confusion written on his face like a poem.

"Your... dealing thing. The weed. How does it connect to the pizzas? And the pancake?"

"What bloody pizzas or pancakes? Paul, what are you talking about?"

No, we spoke of this. I'm sure we did. He trying to call me daft? Forgetful? No.

"No. But, I—we talked about—"

"Sorry, Paul," Stephen shrugged.

Bloody hell. He's told me something, but not enough. How do I apply pressure? Should I? What gives me that right?

"You deal to kids. Talk or I do. Easy."

"No! You—I'll—if they find out they... they..."

"They bloody what? Speak, man!" I yelled.

106

He throws up out me window again. Swear that was half a fish finger just gone flying out his gob. Bloody hell.

"I've said enough. You know I'm trapped and you know why. Leave it alone, Paul. He's bloody dangerous."

"Who's blo—"

Nope. He's off. Door open, wandered off. How's he meant to get home? His car's at improv and I brought him here. Where does he think he's going?

Wait, what is—what—

"STEPHEN!" I yell, but it was already too bloody late.

Bloody late-night bloody lorry driver bloody blood everywhere—

Pancake.

Dick pancake.

Stephen pancake.

Chapter 16 - Fish fingers and Pancakes

See blue lights. Feel cold bench. Taste blood in the air.

Stephen pancake. Stumbled off, into the road, drunk as a bloody skunk. Cuddle with a lorry.

That poor bloody lorry driver. He'll be haunted by that rest of his days. Least Stephen has someone else to haunt instead of me. Selfish thought but can't be dealing with more ghosts.

I should get up and go talk to him, really. Sat there sobbing over Stephen pancake. Bit bloody unprofessional, that.

But can't seem to get my knees to agree with me, gripping my steering wheel like throttling a villain.

Looks like he's called it in. Blues and twos. Wonder what that means, anyway? Still, the old bill are here now.

Almost feels like I'm watching a skit here. Drunk teacher, stumbling into the road. Lorry driver, on your bloody phone, bloody liability. Action.

Fish fingers and pancakes. Stephen pancake. Bloody hell, better not loiter behind my eyes like a Dick pancake.

Probably not. Never really liked Stephen. Didn't deserve to become a crash test dummy turned pancake, but still. Bit of a tosser, dealing dope to kids.

Right, well. Seems I've got to talk to these bloody uniformed officers now. So bloody unprofessional.

Yes, sir, I saw what happened. Yes, sir, that's his bloody half-eaten fish finger and vomit on the floor. Yes, sir, he was drunk as a bloody monk. No, sir, I'm fine as shandy. Didn't say anything, sir. I ain't bloody trusting these bloody unprofessional police. No chance.

Bloody sobriety test. Don't even drink. Bloody late for improv now. Bloody ridiculous. Bloody fish fingers and pancakes.

Right then. Let's just forget about Stephen pancake, shall we? Go have some fun.

Hop in my car, Stephen next to me. Wait no, no he's bloody not. He's bloody pancaked under a lorry. Still got his stupid happy meal box here though. Can't be unhappy with a happy meal, that's what Dick always said. Or was that Stephen?

Off I go then. They don't need me anymore. Done my bit. Might be able to catch the last of improv.

Back to improv, Stephen noticeably absent. Car still here though. Where was he?

Bugger. They're winding down. There go the stragglers. Bloody hell. Missed my weekly therapy session.

Not therapy, bloody improv. Fish fingers and pancakes.

"Paul? You alright?" Hannah rushing over.

Barely remember getting out my car, much less driving here.

"You're crying, and is—is that a happy meal?" she gently offered.

"I'm not bloody crying!" I shouted. "Unprofessional!"

She sat me down, chairs nearby. Just Hannah and me here now. Must admit, the seat feels delicious. I think I needed it. Maybe I need my own Happy Meal.

"Paul, what's going on?"

Oh right. Err, I see Hannah, feel the chair, taste the cardboard from the happy meal box—why am I chewing this thing exactly?

"Stephen pancake," I blurt out. "Lorry. Alcohol. Pancake."

"Huh? What are you—"

Colour drains from her face as the headlights hit her in the eyes. Big, bright, beaming headlights shining the truth into her brain like it did my eyes.

Stephen pancake.

Bloody hell, she's sobbing now. Bit unprofessional this. Should I comfort her? Christ, guess her and Stephen were linking hips after all. Or is that bumping? No wonder he looked so bloody tired all the time. Sure she kept him up all day.

"What the hell happened? Did he say anything? What did he say?" she mumbled, wiping away tears.

"Not a bloody thing," I lied. Daren't tell her about the email.

Blackmail, not bloody email. Same thing I s'pose. Still, she didn't need to know. Not like it would stop him cheating on her with that lorry.

"So he just—"

"Stumbled off, drunk as a monk. Stephen, fish fingers and pancakes."

She nodded her head, wiped away her tears and reset her face like a laptop. "Right. I'm going home. You are too. I'm worried about you, Paul. You seem wrong."

Off she hopped. That felt very professional. Christ. S'pose she's right though. Should probably go home. Was going to take Stephen to the Bear's Paw first though.

Oh wait, can't. I can still take his keys though, they're sat in my pocket. Does Stephen actually have any family? He was divorced, I knew that. Don't think he does. He has a twin brother, I think, but he might be fictional. Can't really remember. Maybe it was an improv thing?

Right, think, Paul. Bloody think. In my car now, gripping the steering wheel. I see the happy meal box, keeping Stephen's seat warm, just in case he needs it.

Probably not, though. Fish fingers and pancakes.

I'm home now. Open the door. Mary isn't in her armchair? Must be upstairs.

"Help," I slip. That's not how you bloody say "Hi, love," you bloody muppet, Paul. So unprofessional.

"Jesus!" Mary calls, dropping her tea. Carpet drank it up like a thirsty carp drinks water.

Arm around me, sat me on the sofa. There we go. I see the telly, hear the clock, taste her shampoo. Smell it I mean. Taste salt.

"What happened, Paul? Are you OK?"

Fine as shandy, love. "Fish fingers and pancakes. Stephen pancake," I mumble.

Bloody get it together, Paul. So unprofessional.

"What... what happened?" she gently prodded like a taser in the kidney.

"Stephen. Drunk as a monk. Cuddles with a lorry. Pancake."

Don't think I could have made that much clearer. Nice and professional, that.

She hugs me tight, gripping my hand like a sea otter. Not letting me float off in the ocean again it seems. Yeah, I'm happy with that.

"Why?" she gently asked, rubbing my shoulder.

"Emailed drug dealer," I said. "Accident they said. Accident. Accident or sui—fish fingers and pancakes."

Mary nodded, but her eyes were sad. Had I upset her somehow? Not very professional that.

"Get some rest, Paul. I'm ringing the doctors first thing, getting you straight to Sandra. We'll talk about this tomorrow."

"She's bloody expensive," I stated factually.

"Mark's got it. Least he can do for you."

Sodding Mark. Securobloodyguard services. Who cares.

"Nice of him," I say, feeling my eyelids grapple with my tired eyes. Maybe I should sleep. Better not dream of fish fingers and pancakes. Not bloody going through that again.

Chapter 17 - Slip past the Sentinel

"Bloody hell, Paul," Sandra said, leaning forward in her chair. "That's terrible. I'm so sorry you had to see th—"

"Cool as a cheesecake," I cut her off like a cat. Domestic short-hair tabby cat, to be specific. Spot of ginger, loves chasing birds. Wonder—

"Paul?"

"Bloody hell, sorry, Sandra. I was off with the cats there. Or the aliens, can't remember."

Sandra sighed, offering me a warm smile. I daren't accept it, feels expensive. Too bloody unprofessional.

"You're dealing with trauma, Paul. You actually saw—"

"I'm fine as shandy—"

"Paul, you're cutting me off and losing yourself in fantasy. You need to process—"

Process? Do I look like a bloody laptop to you, Sandra? Bloody hell. I didn't even like Stephen, hardly gonna cry over the weed-dealing email-sending tosser, am I?

Fish fingers and pancakes.

"So that's our plan. Can you manage that, Paul?"

Bloody hell. I heard about four words. No, more like two. More pills.

"More pills, got it."

Shook her head. "Yes, more pills, more therapy, keep up your gr—"

There were times where I wished that inter-galactic sentient cheesecake would just fly right down and whisk

115

me away like an egg omelette. Bloody boring all this unprofessional touchy-feely therapy.

"Paul?"

"Heard every word," I said, meaning it. Probably.

"Right. Well, we've got plenty more sessions booked and I'll dispense your—"

"Great, great. Need to go now, Sandra. See you at improv," I say, standing to shuffle out the room.

Know what would make this room better, brighter? Disco ball. Just imagine the lights in here, shining, dancing everywhere, cheesecakes and stars around. Maybe—

"See you soon, Paul," Sandra prompted.

Bloody hell, got the prompt but not the character. Should I ask?

Fluorescent light, buzzing loudly in my ears and eyes. Sandra's strawberry perfume. Right. Therapy and pancakes.

Off I shuffle to my car. No, Mary's car, actually. Offered to drive, clean the office later. Kind of her, really. Bloody professional, my wife.

"Got your pills, Paul?" she gently asked whilst sat next to me. Bloody hell, that was fast. Unless I dozed off in the car of course. Wouldn't be the first bloody time.

"Thanks, love, I think so. Wait, pharmacy isn't open on a Saturday?"

"It's Monday, Paul."

Bloody hell. What did I even do with Saturday and Sunday then? Books?

Right, right. Seat belt, Mary's smile, cool cucumbers—

Bah. Not bloody helping today.

Oh! I recall now. Christ, really need to catch up on my sleep. Project Pizzas and Pancakes. Mary and I, in the study, cracking on with the bloody case.

We've really gotten it together now. It's all connected. We know Jake and Paul are—

Jake and Brian, that is. I'm bloody Paul. Really need some water, maybe a cup of tea. Probably some water, too.

116

Seems we've pulled into home now. Barely noticed us leaving the doctors surgery.

"Get some rest, Paul," Mary suggested suggestively.

"S'pose I should. Then it's back to the pizzas and pancakes?"

"Yeah. It is," she muttered. Cool like the cucumber, my Mary. Right then. Off to bed, lay a bit, rest my eyes.

Nice and easy to sleep with this ocean of pills I'm taking. No Stephen or Dick pancakes behind my eyes either. Just nice, calm, cool, calculated sleep.

Bloody hell. Open my eyes, and birds are chirping. Or is it tweeting? No bloody idea anymore.

"Morning, love," Mary said as she gently stroked my arm.

"Bloody hell, how long was I—"

"Long while. Near enough sixteen hours. Feel better?"

Had to give that some thought, really. Honestly, I think so.

"Not really," I slipped, tugging at the duvet. "But time to get up."

Got up, dressed. Ate a handful of pecans. Tasted like pecans. More delicious than this pen in my study, definitely.

"So I've been at work in here, Paul, last night and earlier this morning. I've written down what we know, what we don't, and what—"

Bloody professional, my Mary. The way she thinks and feels, her gorgeous hair. Not even sure what colour you'd call it. Silver blonde? Reminds me of a cheesecake I once—

"Focus, Paul." Snapped me to attention like a twig.

"Sorry. I'm listening," I stated honestly. Probably.

"Bear's Paw may be connected. Spicy Pizza Palace, too. They've a driver called Darius, and—"

I've heard that before somewhere, haven't I? Spicy palace? Pizza? Wasn't tubby getting pizzas delivered to the school from Newcastle? And they came with oregano or basil, I'm sure of it. Bloody herb.

"Paul," Mary clicked her fingers at me like a light switch. Bloody hell, can't seem to focus today.

Fortunately I've a cup of tea. Not that I can recall making it, but Mary did shuffle off for a minute or sixty.

"So, key players I think," Mary began. "Darius, Jake, Brian—"

All these names were getting boring. I already knew all this. Wait, did she name more than three? Bloody hell, this is getting frustrating. Not very professional at all.

"Sorry, can you repeat that, love?" I meekly mumbled.

"Yeah. Spicy Pizza Palace, Bear's Paw, and the Fensham Farm, isn't it?"

"Is that what it's bloody called? I can't remember. I just call it the farm," I admitted. "Easier."

Mary glared. "Paul, we live in bloody Norfolk."

"So?"

"It's all fucking farms!" Mary blurted, laughing out loud.

Bloody hell! I've never really heard Mary swear before. I think? Can't remember. Might be right, though. Fields around here, flat as a pancake.

Dick pancake. Stephen pancake.

Shook my head, gripped my mug of tea tight. Hand shook a little. Focus.

"So we have six suspects and at least five places of interest," Mary said simply. "Did you catch all that?"

"Like a Frisbee, love," I said, on it like a cat's bonnet. Got the lot. Probably.

"Mary, I'm bloody frustrated off work. Sandra bloody trying to get me to stay signed off. Not bloody professio—"

"No." Cut me off like a sickle through a sausage. Bugger.

She might be bloody right. Should I really be leaping back into my motor so soon, after seeing some fish fingers and pancakes?

But I do need to do something. I can't just sit here solving puzzles all day, even if I do get to spend time with Mary.

I've got it. I'm not on patrol, don't have my motor, but I've got my mates. I can go see Darren at the storage facility, Claire at... where does she go now? Oh right, she's cover. I think? Bloody hell.

Or Brian or Jake. Bloody stoners.

Darren seems like the right call. He used to be Dick, so he'll understand, I'm sure. Better not be dancing in the moonlight again though. Bloody hell, that'd be unprofessional.

Now how to get out of this house? Need a plan. Something that'll just get me outta here, slip past the sentinel unseen. Think, Paul. You convinced Mary to marry you once. You can convince her to let you out of here. There's got to be a way, just think it through, make a plan and stick to it. Nice and cool, nice and calm, like a cucumber ninja.

"Popping out a bit, love," I state.

"Be safe."

That was bloody close. Nice and professional. Right then, off I go to the storage facility. Fish fingers and pancakes.

Chapter 18 - Additional Training

Right then. Slipped past the sentinel, off to the storage facility in Wisbech. Light on in the guard hut, always a good sign, but no Darren. Out on patrol maybe? Not sure, I'll slip in and have a look.

Must look bloody unprofessional. I'm wandering around on a secure site wearing a ratty old jumper and jeans. Didn't even bring my bloody torch, or a pizza.

Shuffle over to the car park and—oh no. You're bloody kidding me here.

Bloody Darren bloody pancake.

Shake my head, stare again. No he isn't, he's not here. His car is gone, so he's... he's at the bloody Paw? Bloody hell. Do I call him, nice and cool, professional cucumber? Think I do.

Fumble with my phone from my pocket once I'm back at the hut. If he ain't here I might as well be. Right then, nice civil calm chat with Darren.

"Paul? You—"

"Where the bloody fucking hell are you, mate," I snap like a rubber band. "I'm at your fucking guard hut, you to—"

"Shit! Ain't you signed off, Paul? What are you doing ther—"

"What am I doing here? Mate, what bloody AREN'T you doing here? You at the fucking Paw?"

Nice and cool. Nice and professional. Seem to be sweating a fair bit, though, chest feeling tight. Might need to cool it down even more. Cucumbers and pancakes.

He hung up on me. Guess I'll make a nice cup of tea, sit back, wait.

Moments passed and he's pulled in. Bloody hell. Rushing out his motor, sprinting over to see me.

Turn the chair around slowly like a villain, as he crashes through the hut door.

"Good evening, Mr Bond," I joke. "We've been expecting you." Forgot to bring the cat. Do I have a cat?

"Paul, I'm bloody sorry, mate, I can explain—"

"Explain what, mate? That you're bloody unprofessional? Skipping out on site again after I gave you a chance? Dancing in the bloody moonlight, mate," I state simply.

"Sorry, Paul. Look—baby is poorly. Needs an operation. Waiting lists on the—"

"Doesn't excuse it though, does it, mate," slice him off like a pizza. Don't need all that. Too bloody unprofessional.

"No. I guess not. But please, don't—"

"I feel for you, Darren, but way I see it, you got a choice. Report to Mark yourself, or I'll do it."

Darren sighed, clenching his fists.

"Shit. Look, I'll call him and admit it and beg him not to fire me."

"Go on, I'm watching, mate. Ain't too late."

Watch him pull out his phone, hand shaking a little. I'm sure he'll be greeted by the bloody "Mark Holland, Securoguard Services" that we all love hearing so much.

"Yes, sir, I understand. So this... additional training you call it, when does that start? I see... so it's... I—I need the money. Don't suppose I have a choice, do I?"

Bloody boring. Done listening to this crap. Swear I can smell lemon. Air freshener? Lemonade? No idea. Might be imagining it.

Wait, what was all that about? That sounded complicated, didn't it?

Slipped the phone back in his pocket, shoulders slumped. Weight of the world worn on his face like a Dick pancake.

"Well?" I ask expectantly.

"I'm not fired," he mumbled. "But I am reassigned. Additional training, then off to work the farm, it seems."

"Well, least you did the honest thing, and still employed, mate. You're a good man really. Proud of you," I state nice and factual, nice and cool.

Offered me a smile like a limping puppy. "Better leave the site then, Paul," he says, gesturing towards my motor.

Right then. That's that sorted and I'm off back to slip in past Mary. See what she's been up to. Can't know I've been out. Probably? Probably.

Right. Home now. Need to slip back in past the sentinel. Quiet like a ninja, cool like a ginger tabby cat hunting a bird. Can't park on my driveway, Mary will see the headlights. Element of surprise, park across the street, kill the lights. Nice and professional.

Creep up to the front door, though my bloody knees object. Just like the tabby cat, stalking my own bird. Right then. Feels tense, but I'm ready to slip back in. Key in the lock, nice and quiet, slow turn. No creaking or squeaking, thank Christmas. In I go, slip past Mary and—

"Hi, Paul, you OK?" she says, standing in the kitchen, arms folded.

"Fine, love, just back from seeing Darren. How are you?"

Mission accomplished. I feel like a secret agent over here. Or a ninja cat with a cucumber.

"Good, thanks. How is he?"

"Bloody dancing in the moonlight again. Bloody unprofessional, that," I stated like a snake slithering.

"Reported him. Well, reported himself, but I made him do it."

"Ah, working at the pub you mean? Like last time?"

"Yeah, love. He's been reassigned now, to the farm. Additional training."

"Not fired? What additional training?"

Mary sat beside me on the sofa. She seemed very interested. So professional. Wait a minute—that's a bloody good question actually. What additional pancakes? I never got any on my farm shift. Did I miss something here? And why wasn't he fired? Abandoned his sodding post!

"Paul?"

"Fish fingers and pancakes," I blurt out.

"Think you need some rest, Paul," Mary states.

Maybe she's right. Have been through a lot recently. Pretty tired of pancakes, that's for sure. Guess I can ask about the additional fish fingers tomorrow.

Do fish even have fingers? Unprofessional that.

Chapter 19 - Moonlight and Mushrooms

Answer your bloody phone, Mark. Securobloodyguard services. I've called him twice and he isn't picking up. What's the big idea here?

Late morning already and I'm sat across from Mary, cups of tea at the study desk. Can't really follow what she's working on, all these pills and ghosts. Frustrating, that.

Feels like I'm onto something but it's just out of reach. Might need to buy a step ladder.

"No luck, Paul? He might be busy. He's seemed stressed at the office lately," Mary mused, amusing me.

Bloody funny she was.

"Bloody Mark. Securobloodyguard Services!" I chuckled.

Don't think she got the joke. Flew right over her head like a salmon upstream.

"Still, think you're right. It's odd that he didn't fire Darren. Didn't he fire Brian years ago for moonlighting?"

Bloody good question that. Christ, we're talking years ago now. Need to think. Ah! Yes! The bloody mushroom place with all the mushrooms.

"He did!" I blurted. "But he's a mushroom now."

"Try that again, Paul," Mary gently suggested. Mustn't have heard me. Clearly getting old.

"Moonlight and mushrooms," I began. "But he's back now. Mark rehired him a while ago."

"He did? Something feels strange. We should investigate."

"We're like Sherlock and Holmes," I aptly said.

"Watson," Mary groaned.

"What's on what, love? Telly? Those bloody soaps you love," I chuckled as she glared at me. Oops. Better be professional.

"Why do you love those things so much anyway?" I asked, warm smile, cool cucumber.

"For a long while, Paul, you haven't really... been here. Out working twelve-hour nights, with twelve-hour days in your study."

She looked at me. Right into me. Proper staring into my soul here like the man in the mirror with his Happy Meal box.

"They gave me the drama I was lacking. The wine, the escape. But sat across from you here, now? I—"

She's honestly getting a bit too touchy-feely for me here. Need to go buy her a cheesecake. Or a... wait! I got it!

"I love you, Paul," she concluded, smiling like a salmon.

"Love you too. Right, love, get your coat on. Let's go out for lunch. Stop in and have a chat with Securobloodyguard Mark. Need to ask him about those dutiful pancakes."

Grabbed our coats and off we went. Today wouldn't be boring, was bloody sure of that.

Let Mary drive. Had to be honest, wasn't fully feeling myself. Was feeling my knees, though, bloody things.

Pulled into the industrial estate, office open. Bloody hell, need to get in there fast. Rush into the office, knees be damned, and calm down this little riot.

"Bloody hell, Brian," I say, bursting into the office. "Calm yourself down, mushroom man."

"Stay out of this, Paul," Brian threatened like an overdue bill. Bugger, I need to pay my council tax. Bloody taxman, always wanting my tax.

"Mark here needs to learn himself some manners. No respect, none at all." Brian was hovering over the desk, looked ready to beat Mark into a fine paste and serve him on a piece of toast.

"We're all adults here, Brian," I stated, cool and cucumber. "What's going on then? Let's work this out. No need for any more pancakes."

"Fuck you, Mark. I quit. Paul, get help, you crazy old bastard."

Just like that, Brian fled the scene like a burglar. Bloody hell, think he socked Mark one—bugger got a swollen lip.

"Mark, mate, Brian said you need help. What's going on?"

"I'm fine, Paul, don't worry. He was unprofessional anyway, don't know why I ever hired him back. Hello, Mary," Mark explained. Well, that explained all that then. Nice and sorted, cool and cucumber.

"Mark, may I ask you something?" Mary said.

"Sure he's busy, love. Let's just—"

"Go for it, Mary." He cut me off like a cheese wire through a cheesecake.

"Darren was moonlighting, putting you in breach of contract with the storage company. Why not fire him?"

"Green goblins," I helpfully added.

"Sit down, Paul. Here."

Mary handed me a delicious tasty treat. A pen I could chew on. Nice bit of hard plastic. That'll keep me nice and busy whilst she talks to Mark. Probably.

"Honestly, it's my business, and I don't have to explain myself to a part-time cleaner."

That was bloody professional. Not like Mark—he's normally so touchy-feely. Wonder why the pens with the red lids taste better?

"You don't, no. But I'm asking. Are you OK? Is something going on?"

The smile on his face flipped upside down. Silly Mark, wearing it the wrong way. Doesn't even know how to smile properly yet running a big security company. Fish fingers and pancakes.

"Nothing I can't handle, Mary. Thanks for the concern. I'll see you tomorrow," he said, gesturing towards the door.

Offered me a wounded smile as I stood, groaning. Seemed sad to see me, somehow. Had I done something to upset him? Didn't matter really. Mark and I are old school, we don't need to feel things.

"Feel a bit better after that, don't you, love?" I said to Mary as we drove to the... I forgot to ask where we were going. Oops.

"Not really, Paul. He's clearly under some kind of pressure, but I'm not sure why. Do you still have Brian's number? That seemed... important."

"I do, actually," I helpfully replied. "His lucky number is twelve. Mine is cheesecake."

That should help.

Mary sighed, taking my phone from my pocket once we pulled up at the café.

"Here it is. Thanks, Paul," she said, handing me back my phone. Guess I should give her back the pen, since we're trading.

"That's fine, love. What's for lunch?"

"I'm not sure. But I'm hoping Brian is hungry," she responded.

Well, that made no bloody sense. Do I need to wait for Brian to be hungry before I can eat now? Honestly, Mary, the things she comes out with sometimes. Doolally.

Still, I need some food. Haven't eaten properly since fish fingers and pancakes. Wandered out into the road, drunk as a monk, pancaked by a lorry. I bet he won't make that mistake again. Bloody teacher should have known you can't hug lorries.

Mary got me a full English, sat together at our table, corner of the café. Hardly anyone here, bloody nice, quiet. Romantic even. Or maybe the word was professional.

"Feeling any better, Paul?" she asked, smiling softly at me.

"A good meal helped. Been through a lot latel—"

Cut myself off like a knife through a cheesecake. Don't need all that. She gets the point.

"Yeah. You really have. But I'm here for you, we're going to get you well again, and figure out what's going on with Mark. Think it's clear he has secrets, Paul."

She had a point. Wonder what Mark's secret number was, if Brian's was twelve? Think of the devil.

"Sorry about earlier," Brian said, pulling up a chair. "I got a bit heated."

"Brian, mate, do you remember the generator?" I said, instantly earning a glare.

"I was twenty and freshly licenced, mate. Just let it go, Paul. Christ, you're annoying. One minute you're bloody Einstein and the next my granddad is more aware than you."

Was I supposed to know his granddad or something?

"You clearly didn't get that, Paul. He's dead as a dodo, mate. I'm saying you have days where you're bloody slow."

That makes no sense, does it? I'd know if I was dead. Muppet.

"Brian, appreciate you coming," Mary began, handing me the delicious pen back. "We're worried. Are you OK? What's happening with Mark?"

Brian placed his palms flat on the table and sighed. "Wish I bloody knew. He's been training me to work two bloody jobs at once, I've been delivering pizzas on my shifts too."

He leaned in close before continuing. "But only ever one or two a night and only to certain pl—"

"Pizzas and pancakes," I added, cutting him off.

"Hush, Paul. Let the man speak."

Bloody hell. I'm sure I have something to add here, but what is it? A recipe of some kind, I think? Think, old man. Bugger.

"I don't get it, but, police took an interest. But there was nothing special about it, truly, it was just pizza. Ate a slice myself even."

"No cannabis?"

Brian raised an eyebrow. "Cannabis? Paul, you got a new err... hobby, mate?"

"No no no," I groaned. "In the pizza box."

"Cannabis in a pizza box? Paul, mate, I was kidding before, but I mean it now. Get help."

I don't understand. He wants me to get help. Maybe Mary?

"Can you help me please, Mary?" I asked gently.

"Of course, dear. Go to the car, I'll be with you in a minute. Love you."

Right then. Back to the car, leave the mushroom man to chat to the missus.

That was odd. Why was Brian told to deliver pizzas? Why was there no weed? Was he lying? A decoy? A trap? Something felt off here and I needed to talk to someone about it.

Plain old boring pizza. I thought police were meant to like doughnuts, not pizza.

Bloody hell! Car door woke me. Dozed off in passenger seat, Mary back beside me.

"Mushroom man left?" I asked her. Looks like she's seen a ghost.

"Yeah. He did."

"You OK, love? Looking pale as the moonlight," I suggested.

She smiled back at me. "Poetic for you, Paul. Brian told me Mark owns the Bear's Paw and the Spicy Pizza Palace. Isn't that... interesting?"

"Wow!" I blurted. "Bloody hell, Mark. Good for him. Not that long ago, he was punching pennies. Claire told me."

Mary nodded. "Yeah. Is a little off, isn't it. I'm taking you home to get some rest, Paul. Then I need to go... clean the office."

Bloody professional, my wife. Rest might not be a bad idea, honestly. I'm knackered.

∞

"So Mark owns the pizza shop now? Bloody professional, isn't it?"

Mary narrowed her gaze. "Gotta go," she pops like a toaster.

"Where?" I inquire.

"Office. Cleaning, remember? Get some rest," she abruptly erupts and off she goes. She did mention that before. Probably.

Well, not a bad idea maybe. Just sit in her chair a minute or two. Bloody hell, can see why she likes this thing so much, I'm falling asleep just sitting here—and that's without the bloody wine.

"Hi, Paul!"

Bloody hell! Is that—there's no bloody way. It's a sentient bloody cheesecake! No way! No sodding way!

Look at the glorious bastard. Lemon, too, with a great big bloody smile. Bloody hell, he's majestic. Floating there grinning at me, happy as Larry, shining like a beacon in the dark.

Right. Grounding. Almost forgot about this. Armchair, telly, tea—

"Relax, Paul, you're fine. Not banoffee, just dreaming," Gary said.

Phew, that was a relief. How'd I know his name was Gary anyway?

"Gary's my favourite name," I told him. "If I had a son, I always planned to call him William."

"Makes sense," Gary said, lemon scent permeating my eyes as he did. "I'm here to help you, Paul. Got your eyes on backwards, mate."

"With what? I don't need help from a bloody cheesecake, mate. Nice and prof—"

"Professional? Give me a break, mate," Gary cut me off like a cheesecake through a knife. "You're missing what's right in front of you, doddering old git. Mark's as crooked as a ruler, and you can't bloody see it."

"Rulers are straight as an edge, mate," I retort. "You're bloody bananas Gary."

"I'm obviously lemon you nitwit. Ruler ain't straight if it's made out of rubber is it Paul?"

Bloody hell. Gary had me there. Was Mark a rubber ruler? Shit. It made sense, though, didn't it? So many guards implicated, the additional training, the weed pizza, the stoners, the—

"Paul, mate, kinda busy here. You mind waking up for me so I can bugger off?" Gary cut me off like a cheesecake through a fork.

Snored myself awake, gripping the arms of Mary's chair tight. Right, well, that was—what was that?

Think I need to buy some cheesecake from the corner shop. That'll help. Maybe share some with Mark. Crooked Mark. Drug-dealing, dope-slinging, pancake-flipping Mark.

Fuck.

Well, that was heavy. Finally got to meet Gary though. Been hovering around up there a long while, hiding out amongst the stars.

Feel like I need to pay my respects somehow. Knees argue with me as I bound towards the corner shop.

"Jayir, mate, got any lemon cheesecake?" I say, bursting through the door.

"Mr Paul! Long time, sir, long time. Yes, sir, is in fridge."

Lovely. Right then, let's go have a look. Bloody legend, Gary—found a nice little lemon cheesecake here just like you. Tap the plastic, trot you right on back home.

Dick pancake. Stephen pancake. Gary cheesecake.

Ticking clock, soft chair, tart taste of lemon in my mouth and my nose. Gary somehow seemed sweeter in my dream, but bloody delicious all the same.

"To your honour, Gary. Thanks for the rubber ruler, mate," I announced, finishing the last of my cheesecake.

Felt more awake, more alive, more present than I had in days, lemon sparking my tongue and brain to life.

Still foggy, but Gary was a lighthouse for my train lost at sea. Back on the track now, though the mist persisted.

Mark is a crooked bastard. Straight as a rubber ruler. Owns the distribution network outright. Impressive for a man pinching pennies.

I have Stephen's bloody car keys. Is his car still there? Is his phone in the car, with evidence of the email? Or was it blackmail?

Darren. Farm. Additional training, additional containers. Dick pancake.

I need to see what's in Stephen's car. I need to see what's in those containers at the farm. I need to find a way to tell Mary, before the fog of war obscures my vision once more.

Can't count on Gary to come through for me again. I'm sure sentient cheesecakes are busy with cosmic quests. Probably.

"I'm home, Paul," Mary stated, joining me on the sofa.

Don't remember bringing myself to the sofa, but can't deny that I'm here. Pen and paper, maybe? Write down the thoughts? Delicious pen?

"I met Gary!" I yelled happily.

"Um... Paul? Who is Gary?" Mary asked.

Oh right. That needs context. Probably.

"Sentient cheesecake, love. Lemon, actually. Always thought he'd be banoffee to be honest."

Mary frowned, concern painted on her face like the remnants of a lemon cheesecake.

"He told me something. Mark is as crooked as a rubber ruler, love."

Mary focused on me. Studied me, really looking at me.

"Paul, are you—"

"More myself than I've been in weeks, Mary. Mark owns the bloody distribution ring. He's running the operation. Darren's at the farm with those containers. I need to see what's in them."

Mary sat down slowly. Still watching me, weighing whether this was clarity or cheesecake.

"Tell me about Gary," she said carefully.

"All started with your bloody magic armchair, love. Fell asleep, he flew on by, woke me up clear as crystal."

Mary nodded. "Paul, you aren't magically past your trauma, but I see the focus. Maybe your new meds are fina—"

"Never mind all that," I said, cutting her off like cheese through a cake. "Containers at the farm. I still have Stephen's bloody car keys. Mark is...Mark's a tosser!"

Nice to see Mary laugh out loud again. Been a while. Seemed she agreed.

"You're in no position for risking your neck, Paul, or seeing that farm again. You'll not go."

How could I not? There was no way. I needed to. Gary willed it. The truth demanded it. I was going.

"OK, love, I'll leave it be. What's on the telly?" I protested fiercely.

"No idea, but we'll find something."

Clicked through a bunch of boring flashing lights on a box, sounds blaring out of it. Still, I couldn't think about anything else. Darren's face laughing as I stared at the containers. What mysteries lay within? I must know. Dick demanded it.

Good. Mary cracked open the red. Won't be long, now, and she'll doze off. Then it's time for a secret mission.

Gary and container cake.

Ah bugger. Old habits, though, isn't it? I'm being a rubber ruler myself. Ignore Mary, let her drink into a wine coma and bugger off to the farm. Exactly where I promised I wasn't going. Promises aren't pancakes—Mary deserved professionalism.

"Mary, love," I slipped out. Still time to bite your tongue, old man, stay professional. Best not share.

"I can't let this go. I need to see those containers."

Mary frowned. She stood, putting her wine bottle back in the cold cupboard, and sat next to me.

"Can't talk you out of this, can I? We don't know how dangerous Mark actually is, Paul."

"Or how desperate Darren is," I added.

"Right. And be honest, since this whole thing started— where is Jake?"

Bloody good point. Hadn't seen the bloody sto—dirty drug-dealing pizza pusher once.

"I'm staying here, phone at the ready. You be bloody careful. Don't get caught or hurt," Mary demanded.

"Don't worry, love," I whispered, "proper cucumber cat ninja me."

Right then. It was getting late, and I'd soon have a secret mission on my hands. Sure hope Gary had my back—things were getting tense over here.

Chapter 21 - James Bond

Secret mission time, Agent Paul Hope reporting for duty.

Made sure I'm dressed in all black for the occasion, nice and stealthy, cool like a cucumber ninja. There's a rubber ruler at this farm, and I'm going to sneak in and find it. In those bloody containers, I'm sure of that.

I'm wearing all black, though, so bit of a safety hazard. Made sure to also wear a hi-vis jacket with reflective stripes, make sure I don't hurt myself.

Tap my finger fast against the steering wheel, approaching the farm. Not feeling very professional, for some reason. Am I missing something here?

I'm off to see Darren, at the farm, with additional pancakes. There are new containers at the farm, locked up tight. Also a harvester I need to question—he is the star witness after all, but I'd need to be careful—he's proven to be bloody dangerous.

Right then. Best kill my headlights as I approach. I can just about see the guard hut, and Darren isn't in it.

Let's park next to him. He's in Dick's spot so I'll just park behind him. He won't suspect me if he can't leave.

Bright light from the guard hut called out to the darkness, a beacon of light and hope. Almost like Darren at the storage facility, with those green goblins. Where was he, anyway?

I best be careful, make sure he doesn't see me. Slip past the hut—he isn't here, which is good. There's the barn, the storage shed, few tractors—I'm on the right path.

Right then. I can see Darren now, so I'm doing well. This is going brilliantly. Darren's boots squelched in the mud as he waved his torch around near the fence. Can't let him see me until I've questioned the star witness.

Slip into the barn. Showtime.

"Right you," I mumble to the harvester. "I know you're bloody up to something. Why'd you kill my friend Dick?"

Silent treatment. Right, how to apply a little pressure? What's a harvester afraid of, anyway? Mechanics?

Bet his name is Harvey. If I owned a cat I think I'd—

"What the bloody hell are you doing here, Paul?" Darren said, startling me. Christ.

"Darren! Sorry, I'm uh, look, mate."

Can't let him know I'm here to question the star witness. Bloody hell, get it together, Paul. It's a bloody harvester. Smell of Darren's cologne, bright light from his torch, mud under my boots—

"Paul? What the hell?"

"Right, right. Sorry, mate. Off with the cheesecakes there. Bloody hell, how'd you even see me?"

Darren sighed. "You're wearing a fucking hi-vis jacket, mate? And you parked behind me?"

Bugger. Darren was no fool. That additional training had made him very professional.

"Look, you got me," I begrudgingly admitted. "But you know what's going on here, Darren. Mark is bent as a rubber ruler, mate, Gary told me."

"I don't know who—look. I'm supposed to report trespassers, Paul, and you've no business need to be here."

"I need to question the star—"

No. Wait. That's wrong. Harvey wasn't going to help me.

"Containers. Let me see inside them."

Darren glared right into my brain. Felt off, somehow. Seemed angry.

"No. Get out of here before I report you like you did me, Paul."

Bloody hell. He has to know what he's doing, doesn't he? He's smart. Additional training.

"Darren," I said gently, smiling warmly at him. "Those containers—what's in them?"

"You bloody know what's in them, Paul," he harshly replied. "Because of you, I'm stuck here, taunted by them. I need the money. You can't see them. Just go."

Shook my head, trying to shake out the disappointment, but it just wouldn't leave.

"What kind of father do you want to be, Darren?"

"Fuck off, Paul."

Darren stomped away to the hut, pointed to my car. Fine, then—seems I'm to leave. Open the door to his guard hut, need to give him a nice cool professional chat.

"I'm sorry, Darren," I admitted. "I regret reporting you. But you betrayed me, too, mate."

"Paul, don't you think I bloody know that? I'm thinking about my baby, mate. Then you go and tell me what bloody kind of dad—look. Look, Paul."

Darren stood, sighed, hand on my shoulder. Felt warm despite the cold of night.

"I'm sorry I swore at you. I never saw you here. You need to leave—now."

There we go then. Smooth as salmon, mission successful. I've confirmed the containers are full of pancakes—at least, I think I have? I've also confirmed Harvey killed Dick. Bloody harvester, meant to gather crops not make pancakes. Leave the kitchen to the chefs.

Made my way back to the car, pulled off. Promised I'd call Mary, didn't I? Best do so.

"Hi, love," I said, her answering on the second ring. Made sure to use the hands-free, not bloody safe to use the mobile on the road. Not even wearing my hi-vis jacket—last thing I needed was more pancakes.

"Paul?"

141

"Sorry, love, missed that. I saw Darren. He said the containers are full."

"Full of what?"

"Didn't say."

Heard her sigh down the phone. Must be tired, bless her. She does worry about me a lot. Should buy her a Gary or something.

"Get home safe, Paul."

"Will do. Love you, Mary," I stated simply.

"Yeah. Love you too."

Right then. It's off to the corner shop, if it's still open, then the study with the wife. It's been a good day.

Chapter 22 - Off With the Pancakes

"Paul, you're home," Mary said, smiling warmly at me as I snuck inside.

"Mission was a complete success," I happily declared, taking off my sodding muddy boots. Those will be a bugger to clean—how do farmers put up with this day in day out?

"Right. So what did we learn then?" Mary mumbled.

"Darren is involved," I stated. "Told me I know what's in the containers. So we're right. It's—"

"Drugs."

"Drugs! Bugger me, that's a wild accusation, Mary!" I exclaimed, shocked to my floor.

"Well it wasn't going to be cheesecake, was it, Paul?"

"Bugger! Left Gary in the car!"

Rushed outside, grabbed the lemon cheesecake, knees be damned.

"Paul?"

"Present for you, love. Enjoy," I said, handing her the cheesecake and a straw.

"Um... thanks, Paul," Mary said, grabbing herself a spoon from the drawer. Weird way to eat a cheesecake but who am I to judge.

"So Darren is compromised, as we feared," Mary said, mouth full of Gary.

"Yeah. Not very professio—"

"Paul. Enough with the professionalism thing. It got boring a while ago."

Boring? That's bloody unprofessio—ah, maybe she's right. Usually is, about most things. Can't admit that, though—not bloody professional.

"He told me I know what's in the containers. I tried to cross-examine the harvester, but he was cold and quiet, like a big lump of metal."

Mary laughed out loud. "Oh, Paul. I do love your sense of humour, even during something serious."

I had no sodding idea what she was banging on about, but I couldn't ignore that smile.

"Well... what do we do next, Paul?"

Felt in my pockets, see if I could find some notes or some kind of clue. Nothing. Just my keys, half a packet of mints, a chewed pen and Stephen's car keys.

"Er, Paul?" Mary asked. "Why do you have two sets of keys?"

"Oh don't worry," I explained. "Just hanging onto those for Stephen pancake."

"Bloody hell!" Mary exclaimed. "You said he was blackmailed?"

"I don't know his email address," I sadly shared. "But I've got his keys here, and I don't think he'll be needing them. Should we go check his car for evidence of blackmail?"

Mary nodded enthusiastically. "Yes. Let's do that, Paul."

Scene: off to the community centre to check out Stephen pancake's car. Prompt: married couple on a secret mission. Action.

Didn't take us long to reach the community centre. Wouldn't be smelling of much tonight, though. Fairly sure it was only Monday, but honestly, who sodding knows at this point.

Stephen's car sat there, same spot as Friday night, staring at me as I stared at it. Almost felt like it wanted to ask me something.

"Poor Stephen," Mary mumbled quietly.

144

"No sense crying over spilt kidneys," I blurted. Bloody hell, that wasn't very kind of me.

"Be kind, Paul. Keys please?"

Stephen, stumbling. Lorry, loud. Person, pancake.

Christ. Came flooding back in like a river of blood, staring at his sodding Mercedes. How'd a teacher afford this thing anyway? Oh right. Private school. Dealing dope to rich kids too. Right, right. Did he name this car? Probably called it Mercy. Why would he try to hug Larry the lorry anyway? Was it an accident? Had he sent too many emails?

"Paul?"

"Sorry, love, off with the pancakes."

Popped the key in the lock, opened it up like a Stephen pancake. Tickets on the window, accusing the car of wrongdoing. What had it done wrong? Was it cheating on Stephen with another teacher?

Shook my head, shaking loose the rust and fog. Can't seem to ground myself out here. Community centre feels somehow off, somehow wrong. Think I want to go home.

"Mary, can we—"

"Here we are." Mary brought a phone out of the car. Presumably it belonged to Stephen, though I guess minus a kidney or two now.

"Does that phone belong to the car now? Shouldn't steal, love," I stated.

"Let's go home, Paul. Take a look at this thing."

Well, off we went, leaving Mercy to her shame. Shouldn't have taken Stephen for granted, and maybe you wouldn't have to mourn him, silly motor. Bloody fleeting, this life of ours. Gone one minute, gone the next.

Right then. Mary took us home, though I remember driving. Back indoors, phone to look at. Still had some charge.

"Bugger." Mary groaned. "Locked to his biometrics."

"His biometrics are painted all over the bloody road, love," I stated factually, minus a little salty water fleeing my eyes.

"Ah, it's alright, Paul."

Mary came over, hugged me tight on the sofa. Not bloody professional, this, but I'm not complaining. Seemed alright somehow, like maybe I needed it.

"Right then," I said some time later. "We need a heist. We need Stephen's finger."

Mary glared at me, pushing me away. "No bloody chance in hell, Paul! Are you insane?"

"No, I can't afford it."

"What? You—there has to be another idea, Paul. We're not cutting the finger off a barely assembled corpse."

Dammit, Paul, think. This is your speciality. You know things, understand them, see the puzzles behind the pancakes. Bugger.

"Well, I've got one idea, love, but it's probably stupid."

Mary sighed, shrugging her shoulders. "Go on then, let's hear it."

She sounded exasperated. Or maybe cheese-grated? I don't know.

"Could always ask Gary I guess?"

"Paul, your bloody sentient cheesecake isn't re—"

"Oh not lemon Gary, love. Talking about Stephen's identical twin brother."

"Ste—iden—what??"

"Didn't I mention hi—"

"No you fucking didn't, Paul! What the fuck! Does he even know Stephen is dead?"

"No I doubt it, love. Lives in Swansea. Bloody miles away."

Mary rushed to the kitchen, drank red right out the bottle. Bloody hell. Who ruffled her fish fingers?

"How would we even get him here? Is there a—Paul, I'm feeling stuck."

Hmm. Focus, Paul.

"Guess I could just unlock it with his passnumber? It's just 1234."

Mary stared at me, mouth agape, like she'd seen a bloody Stephen pancake.

"Why did—how do—just give me the bloody phone."

Mary tapped away at the phone like a hoodie hacker leaned over a laptop. Watching her work, eyes focused on the screen, she looked beau—

"Not much of use on here, Paul. Lots of messages deleted, but his call logs were interesting. Seems he called Mark, Jake, and Hannah a lot."

"Makes sense," I said. "Hannah was sleeping with him. Mark is a kingpin, and Jake a bloody stoner. But no calls to Harvey?"

"Forget Harvey. How did Stephen know Jake, Paul?"

Now that was a bloody professional question.

Chapter 23 - Pills and Pancakes

Tuesday. Rested like a bowl of dough, sat on the windowsill cooling like a pie.

Need some coffee. Fog felt extra foggy today. Pills and pancakes.

Think it's time to have a nice, cool, cucumber chat with Mark. He'll be in his office, sat on his paperwork throne, glass office for that open-plan feel. Likes to spy on his staff, watch them like a hawk watching telly.

Need to get him to see some reason. Admit he's a rubber ruler, turn himself in. He may be a bloody tosser dealing dope to teenagers but he's still professional. Probably.

Gripped the wheel tight, knuckles white, knees protesting already. They could shut up—this is happening, whether they want it or not. I'm the one paying the shots and calling the bills here. Bloody knees and their mutineering.

Here we are. Industrial estate, Securobloodyguard Services. Shield logo staring at me like it knew I'd left the sodding oven on.

Did I? Bloody hell. Best ring Mary and let her know. But not yet, she's cooking lunch, and I need to get back in time for fish fingers and pancakes.

She didn't want to stay home cooking. Wanted to come see Mark. But I couldn't put her in danger—she doesn't own a hi-vis jacket, so wouldn't be safe.

Pulled up next to Mark's motor, sleek, polished, black as the cheesecakes in the sky. What did BMW stand for, anyway? Probably something food-related—made sense.

No final protests from the sodding knees—seemed they finally understood the assignment. Bring an end to this whole investigation, nice and cool, nice and cucumber.

Sat in his office as usual, chair, phone, paperwork, laptop. But he looked different, somehow—where once I saw a friend, a boss, a mentor? Now I saw a tosser. A dealer, pushing weed to kids. Bloody stoners.

Marched right into his office, nice and professional, nice and cool. Cucumbers and pancakes. Time for a friendly little chat.

"What in the fuck are you doing, you stupid, arrogant prick?" I calmly stated. Probably.

"Paul? Calm down, mate, what the—"

"Dealing to fucking kids? Are you having yourself a bloody laugh, mate? Well I ain't fucking laughing, am I?"

Nice and cool. Nice and cucumber. Fists clenched, heat rising in chest, volcano moments from eruption.

"I don't know what your—"

"Save it," sliced him off like cheese through a grater. "Call logs. Stephen pancake. The farm, too—I know what's in those containers, Mark. Harvey confessed to everything."

Had him on the ropes, I could tell. His expression showed fear, confusion, maybe panic—finally cornered the rat, right here in his little den.

"Paul, you're not well. You don't know what you're—"

"Evidence. I've got it, mate. You own the distribution network, your pancake deliveries contain weed. You deal to bloody kids, mate. You're pathetic."

Strange. His eyes looked troubled. I wasn't cutting any onions, but he cried all the same. I did use lemon shampoo this morning—maybe he was allergic?

"I'm sorry, Paul. I'm sorry. They made me. I had no—I had no bloody choice. I swear, I didn't know about the kids, I just—"

Bit sodding unprofessional, this. Don't want to hear it all. All these tears and emotions and confessions. Must remember to change my shampoo.

Bugger, I'm missing something here. I need to listen.

"You're right. About it all, Paul. Jake and Darius deliver the pizzas and I just... I just do as I'm told."

"Jake? Bloody stoner," I mumbled.

"You don't get it, Paul. I own the businesses, I own the distribution network, but Jake? Jake owns me."

"No, mate, slavery has been illegal for a long time in the UK. That's bollocks," I corrected. Bloody hell, think I should suggest Mark see Sandra too. Clearly needs the therapy. "So what else are you bloody hiding?"

Mark sighed. "I'm not giving you anything else, Paul. I've said enough. I've been juggling the pieces so long, putting you in places you shouldn't be, I—I think I wanted you to find out. I do."

Clearly needed to give him some more time to work this out. Maybe I should go buy him a Gary? Help him unwind. Get him really talking.

"Business was failing, Paul. Couldn't just give up everything I worked so hard to build. I didn't think anything of it, at first, I..."

Mark trailed off, straightening his tie like a rubberless ruler. His face flattened, his smile vanished like a ghost.

"I've told you enough. Go, Paul."

He was still in there, somewhere. He was a turtle, I was sure, hiding inside his little shell. Kept saying Securoguard Services like some kind of shield against his cowardice. Bloody stoners.

"Mark, go to the sodding police with me," I suggested.

"Can't. It's too late for that, Paul. I'm owned, like property. Just go."

I had to think of something. I needed a plan, a hook, a lure? A moment to connect with him, man to man, to make him see reason. He was going to talk, and I was going to make him. I just needed the right leverage, applied with precision, with professionalism.

"I'll buy you a cheesecake," I blurted.

That should do it. That'll apply the pressure I need, get him compliant. Spill the soup, Mark.

"Oh Paul. You do make me smile. What flavour?"

"Lemon, mate."

"Sorry, Paul—not even for a toffee one. You're on your own."

Bugger. Almost had him there. Seemed I had to visit the Spicy Pizza Palace to get what I needed instead. That was where that Darius driver guy worked. But the slavery angle disturbed me—Jake owned Mark? How? Was it a contract, a mortgage, a marriage?

Couldn't be. Mark was already married, to that bloody Swedish model. Corker, she was. Still, I—

"Paul?"

"Right, sorry. I'll be off then. But I think you're a bloody coward, mate," I simply stated, cool and professional.

"Can't think about it, Paul."

Strange. Why didn't he want me thinking about his cowardice? Was it another clue somehow, another piece of the pancake puzzle?

Still, I'd learned a lot here today. Harvey would have his day in court, and Mark would too. We were close, I knew it—I needed to find that bloody stoner, or Darius. Then get them to go with me to Tom, the detective, so we could finally have that surprise party.

It was finally time to bring this whole conspiracy to flight. Just like a majestic eagle soaring through the sky.

For now, best go home to Mary. Oven was still on, and I should tell her that. Hope she's done cooking.

Gripped my wheel tight, turning into my driveway. Groaned as I dragged my knackered old knees back into the kitchen, finding my wife sat at the table.

Swear she was psychic—oven already off, lunch on the table.

"Welcome home, love," she gently said as she sat me down at the dining table. "So what happened?"

"Worse than we think, love—Mark's a bloody slave. Jake owns him, he said."

Mary raised an eyebrow, staring right through me. Seemed the truth shocked her just as much as it did me. Bloody stoner.

"I think he means Jake is in control, dear. You've taken that litera—"

"I know what he said, Mary. You'll just have to trust me," cut her off like I wanted to cut off Mark's oxygen supply. Leathery, weathered old hands wrapped around his throat, gasping for air, kids all around cheering for me as they threw cannabis leaves like confetti.

Shook the thoughts from my head. Ticking clock, kitchen table, smell of roast for lunch—wait.

Roast for lunch? That seemed... important, somehow. It was all right there—roast potatoes, steamed carrots, sliced chicken and even Yorkshire puddings. Smell of onion gravy wafted right into my nose, invading my senses. Was it looking for answers? Or—

"Dig in, Paul. You look exhausted."

Right. Probably a good idea.

An hour passed, fully replete, opposite sides of the desk with Mary. Study had become our little sanctuary, our lighthouse watching the ocean as it shrank to a lake. Her eyes met mine, felt more like a river.

We sat and talked, linked our clues, looked over our documents and our notebooks and the cheese grater I brought from the kitchen. Seemed it would be helpful, somehow, but I didn't know how just yet.

"So Mark is running things in all but name, with Jake in control. Still, Paul—I can't help but think we're missing something, here?"

Hmm. She was right, but I had to focus and think. My hands placed flat on the desk. Mary, sat across from me, her perfume in my nose and her eyes in my heart.

I've got it!

"Darius!" I yelled, excitedly. "The Spicy Pixie Pizza place man guy."

"That's one of the businesses, isn't it. He's involved too. How do we get to him?" Mary mumbled, studying a notebook.

I needed a plan. We needed to talk to Darius, and it needed to be smart—he couldn't suspect that we were on to him. How could we do it? Talk to Darius without arousing suspicion, lure him to the lion's den?

I had a thought. A plan—cunning and cruel, callous and controlling. A plan so deliciously intelligent and thoughtful I'm amazed it came from me. Not bad for a knackered old security guard.

"I've got it!" I roared like a lion eating a light bulb. "First, we wait until after dark. Then, we approach the Spicy Pasta Palace with a bent coat hanger—I saw one used as a lockpick in a movie once. Then—"

"Paul, how about we just order pizza?"

Bloody hell, Mary. And I thought my plans were crazy. Well, in for a penny, in for a pizza I s'pose.

Chapter 24 - Cheese, please

Had to get this right. It was seven in the evening, and there wasn't a tolerance for failure.

My hand trembled, holding the phone to my ear. This was important—it had all been building to this. Pancakes and stoners, cowards and corruption.

Dialled the number, hand shaking as I pressed the button. Mary downstairs, soap on the telly, but didn't seem to need the wine so much anymore.

Here we go. Nice and cool, nice and cucumber. Call connected—showtime.

"Spicy Pizza Palace, take your order please?"

Just like that, we were in. I'd connected to the head of the snake. Or was it a hydra? Had to get this right, there was no room for error, no room for failure. Needed to—

"Hello?"

"Sorry, love, sorry," I said, regaining my focus. "Order pizza, please."

"What kind?"

Bloody hell. I knew this would be tough, but I began to sweat under the stress. I just need to relax, breathe, and focus. I'm trained for this. I'm cool like a... cucumber?

"Sir, we don't sell cucumber pizzas. Nobody does. Now what's your real order please?"

Bloody hell, a cucumber slipped past the gate again. Thought I'd beaten that.

Study desk, hand on it. Smell the musk of old books in the air. See the lamp, casting a dim light across the desk in the dark.

Right. The questions were hard, barriers to entry, blocking me from my goal. But I was Paul Hope, and I would have my pizza.

Pizza. What kind? Large, I s'pose, Mary and I can share. But what should it have on it? Should it have pineapple?

That seemed like an incredibly divisive question. Perhaps I'll stick to something simpler.

"Hello?"

"Cheese, please."

"Size?"

"Cheese."

"Right, what size?"

"Cheese. "

Bloody hell, all these questions. Focus, Paul. Mary is counting on you. Everyone is.

"We've established that sir. What size cheese?"

"Extra cheese, please."

"One extra large cheese pizza, great. Anything else?"

Oh dear. I didn't think this far ahead. What do I do?

"Don't know," I admitted honestly.

"Great, great. Address please."

Rattled it off from memory. Only one problem—I gave them bloody Securoguards.

"Sure, that'll be there in half an hour. Twenty quid, cash."

With a click, call was done. I was in, but there were complications. Best inform Mary. Well, wasn't far from us, over in Leverington. Few minutes' drive at most.

"Pizza on the way, love," I said, sitting beside Mary.

"Great. How long?"

"Half hour. Sent him to Securoguard office."

Mary raised an eyebrow. "Uh, why?"

"Didn't want to risk him coming to our home, knowing what we know."

Is that why I did that? Damn I'm clever. Probably.

"Good thinking, dear. I'll get my coat."

"Don't you want to finish watching your soap, Mary?"

She smiled at me, warm like a burger under a heat lamp.

"No. Let's go get our pizza, with a side order of answers."

Damn. Didn't order any of those. Mary would be disappointed.

Ten minutes later, found ourselves pulled up outside the office, industrial estate. Moon smiled at me as the stars twinkled. Sky sure was beautiful, even to knackered old eyes like mine.

You had to wonder what was up there. I was certain the inter-galactic sentient cheesecakes were now at least. Good old Gary.

Still, hadn't met any aliens yet, but there was still time. Night was young, though looking at my gorgeous wife, we certainly weren't. Still, she sure was bloody professional.

"Been a crazy couple months really, hasn't it, Paul?" Mary stated simply.

"Yeah. Feels like I'm having a good day today, love. Somehow feel a bit better after that nice calm chat I had with Mark."

Words spoken, but not felt. Fraudulent like a container farmer growing paranoid teens and pancake harvesters.

Bloody Harvey. Wish we could arrest him right now, but he's the star witness.

Star witness like I witness stars, right now. So bloody professional. Why couldn't I shake that from my head? Hannah laughing, cackling almost, staring at the harvester. What did I see that dug into me like a tubby with a pizza he just wouldn't share?

Was Hannah unprofessional? Something nagged at me. Her shoes? Stephen, something to do with Stephen.

They were sleeping together, I was sure of that. All but confirmed it before he misplaced his biometrics in a lorry pancake. Hope that lorry driver was alright. Doubt he felt very professional after that.

"They're a little late, Paul. But I see headlights. Hop out—see what you see."

Nodded to the wife. The game was on, and the cucumber ninja had a secret mission. Felt the note in my pocket, ready to go. Those same headlights, that same little car as that night I caught Josh with the weed pizza.

Should have just given me a bloody slice, shouldn't he. Could have avoided all this. Wonder if there was pineapple on it?

"Yo, bruv, pizza."

Bloody hell, thing was huge. Don't think we'll finish all that. Reach into my pocket for my master plan, the note, ready to hand it over. Fumbled around for it, pulled it out and gave it to him. Let's see.

"Thanks. Here's your change."

Mission accomplished.

"Wait!" Mary calls out, hopping out the car like a rabbit on a pogo stick. Great, now that's stuck in my head. Boing, boing, boi—

"We know everything. Darius, wasn't it?"

"Yeah, I'm Darius. What do... what do you mean by that, innit?"

Folded his arms like a pancake, glaring at Mary. What was his angle, then? Did he even like pancakes?

"The drugs, Darius. Your boss, Jake. We know it all."

Darius laughed out loud. "Yo, I don't know what you're talking about, love. I deliver pizza, innit. You been watching too many movies."

Mary shook her head. "We know about Jake and Mark. We know."

"You cracked in the head, love? Jake prepares and delivers, but he also working for Mark. He's owner, but he ain't boss."

"Then who is?"

Darius scowled. "Nah, bruv. I've said more than enough. I ain't giving her up. You want answers, go to the Paw on a Wednesday."

Hopped back into his car like a rabbit on a pogo stick, and off he went.

"Damn. Got our pizza, but no answers, Mary. What do we do now?"

"Oh he gave her up perfectly, Paul. He just confirmed it's a woman. Think we both know who."

A woman? Bit bloody unprofessional, that. A woman... let's have a think. Sandra, my therapist? That made zero sense. She was too busy dealing with scrambled eggs and fried noodles.

Claire? The security cover guard. She had full access to multiple sites, knew the business inside and out and often stank of weed—I think? Was it weed or strawberries? Still, it made logical sense that she was involved.

Which meant it couldn't be her. Too clean, too simple. Hannah and the star witness? She was sleeping with Stephen, but the way she looked at Harvey... were they having an affair? Perhaps they were in love? Larry the lorry killed Stephen so they could be together?

But then why kill Dick? What did he know that Harvey needed to kill him for?

I was missing something, I was sure of that. Surely not bloody Mary?

No, Paul, that made less sense than a toaster eating the moon. So who else could it be? Not Hannah, Claire, Mary, or Sandra... that only left...

Jayir's wife! Jurgita! I've only ever met her twice, but she's short. Noticeably short—short enough to run a criminal empire.

"Yeah, love. We do," I said, settling into the passenger seat. Time to go home, a trip to the corner shop in order tomorrow—interrogation, infiltration, and gathering evidence awaited. Mission was bound to be a complete success.

Chapter 25 - Rosemary

Mary isn't convinced, but I bloody was. I was heading down the corner shop, secret mission, hi-vis jacket. Interrogate Jurgita and get her to admit the truth. There were answers to be had, and the questions were hungry. Just lucky she sold crisps, and the occasional Gary.

Surprised Mary couldn't see it. She's the smart one—I'm just the Paul one.

But it made bloody sense. Jurgita sold us all snacks, including frozen pizzas. Knew our names too, and the most damning piece of evidence? She was short. Short enough to run an entire criminal empire, I was sure of that.

I'm on the case, and I'll prove myself right. Jurgita is going down.

Took the motor down the shop. Needed the space for evidence gathering, and my bloody argumentative knees weren't letting me carry it all home.

There was Jayir, stacking shelves like he wasn't husband to a kingpin running a criminal empire. Was he complicit? Had to be—how could she run this right under his nose? Hiding in plain sight, like a Paul in a hi-vis jacket.

Pushed through the front door, bell rang out like a bell ringing. Bloody thing—guess the cucumber ninja approach was off the table then.

"Ah! Mr Paul! Lovely to see you!" Jayir said, smiling warmly.

What lies did he hide behind that warm, caring smile? Only a true professional could find out.

Time to raise the stakes. Cool, calm, interrogation time.

"Lovely to see you, mate," I began. "Do you sell herbs?"

"Of course sir! Many. Oregano, basil, thyme—what you need?"

Bloody hell, it was worse than I thought. They weren't selling cannabis, they were selling TIME itself. How the bloody hell were they doing that?

"Can I, uh, buy some of this... Time? How do you, you know, bottle it?"

"We just order thyme bulk. Same as all other herb, Mr Paul."

Hmm. So it's as easy as that, is it? Who knew. Well then, let's pull at a different thread.

"Do you sell more... specialist... herbs?" I subtly asked. Probably.

Jayir raised his eyebrow. "Like what? Rosemary?"

Damn, he was professional, that was for sure. My cucumber ninja approach didn't seem to be working—what else could I do?

"No, no. I mean like...specialist."

"Dill? Parsley? Sage?"

Bloody hell. I was going to have to be a little more subtle. He just wasn't getting it.

"How about cannabis?" I blurted, nice and subtle like a cucumber ninja.

Jayir's eyes widened. "Of course not sir! No, that would not be legal sir. No no no. Why you asking for this, Mr Paul? Are you in some kind trouble?"

Shook my head like a jazz musician shook the macarenas. "No mate, just wondering, that's all. But say you did, how would you sell it?"

"I wouldn't!"

Bugger, he was a tough egg to crack. Might have been a nut, actually, I forgot. New approach.

"So Jurgita, Wednesday nights, she at the Paw?"

"Oh, yes, of course. Deliver crisps and nuts in boxes. Good customer, very honest. Why, you need her?"

Wasn't ready to go toe to toe with the toepin just yet. But that's how they did it, I was sure—what was the difference between a pizza box and a crisp box to a bit of weed? Nothing! Probably. Right then, time to gather some evidence, the interrogation having gone swimmingly.

"I'd like to buy crisps in boxes please."

"Oh? Bulk buy? Having a party, Mr Paul?"

Blast. I hadn't prepared for the exam again. Really needed to get better at that. What the hell did I say? I suppose I could just tell him the truth?

"Yes."

"Right, OK. What flavour do you want?"

More bloody questions! What was this, a sodding interrogation? Oh wait. That's exactly what this was. Had to think fast.

"Yes."

"Mr Paul? What flavour?"

"Yes. Uh, all. All flavours."

Jayir raised his eyebrow once more. That was smart, get his forehead some exercise. "You want... boxes of all flavour of crisps?"

"Yes, please."

"Huh... some party, must be, Mr Paul?"

"Oh yes, I'm fully expecting to open the boxes and find my herbs. I mean, herbs."

"Uh... right. Well, I help you get boxes to car. Will cost fifty pounds for all these boxes, Mr Paul."

Bloody hell. Gathering evidence sure was sodding expensive. Good job I didn't suspect Gary, or I'd be spending another small fortune on cheesecakes too.

Helped me get the crisp boxes to the car. Mary would be overjoyed once I got home and found them full of time. Or cannabis, whichever really.

"Thanks Mr Paul. Have a good party!"

What bloody party? Was Mary planning me a surprise party? Bugger, how'd he know about that then? He was good. Real bloody good. And he was just the patsy—imagine how smart Jurgita must be.

Never would have suspected these two. Some of the nicest, kindest people I've ever met. So bloody unprofessional that they're kingpins of a drug-dealing operation.

Time to take the evidence home to Mary. I'm sure she'll be happy. Too bad I already know about the surprise party, though—bet it took her ages to plan and Jayir casually spoiled it like a rotten cheesecake left baking out in the sun.

Still, was home now, drive taking seconds. Crisps sat in the back, waiting to be cracked open like eggs full of evidence.

"Paul?" Mary ran over, helping steady me as the boxes fought back. "What the heck did you do?"

"I cracked the case, love. These boxes have evidence on the inside, just like the pancakes."

"You mean the pizzas?"

"Probably."

We cracked open a box of crisps, and nothing could have prepared me for the pure shock that rippled through my very soul.

The boxes were full of crisps. Packets and packets of the things, of all different flavours. Bloody magnificent. There it was, evidence they were dealing crisps, and we had boxes of the things.

No.

That was wrong. I was looking for rosemary.

No! Bloody cannabis. Weed. There wasn't any at all.

Maybe my luck had finally run out. I'd nailed everything so far, every mission a success, every challenge triumphed. I wasn't about to let a bunch of bloody crisps keep me from my prize, and tonight at the Paw? Jurgita was going down. Can't hide that rosemary from me. Probably.

Chapter 26 - Sorry

"Here, love. Got you a Gary."

Placed a lemon cheesecake on the kitchen table, proud, firm, breakfast.

"Thanks, Paul. Interesting choice for breakfast, but let's go for it."

There was that adventurous spirit I married. Dug into our cheesecake, mulling over the morning. Slept like mammals after all that pizza we ate, half the bloody thing still sat humming away in the fridge.

Might have been the fridge humming, actually. That made more sense. Probably.

"Was a very interesting trip to the corner shop," I mentioned, tart lemon dancing with sugar on my tongue.

"Why? And how could it be more interesting than your crispy adventure yesterday?"

"No Jurgita again. Conspicuous by her absence, wouldn't you say?"

Mary raised an eyebrow. "No? What do you mean, Paul?"

"You know... our little investigation, love? Need to get you some coffee."

Times like this I had to smile. Mary didn't do mornings, that's for sure.

"Paul."

"Yes, love?"

"How in the bloody hell did you arrive at Jurgita anyway?"

Oh dear. She had all the puzzle pieces, but she hadn't glued them together like I did. Best get her up to speed.

"So I figure it makes sense, Mary. She's got access to all the snacks we buy as guards, I've only ever seen her twice, and she's the perfect height. Jayir all but confirmed they had rosemary in stock."

Bit early in the morning for her maybe. Looked thoroughly confused like a frog on a fishing boat.

"Or maybe, you know, Claire? Cover guard with full site access? Or bloody Hannah? Sold the farm the harvester that killed Dick? Or he could have lied about it being a woman at all, Paul? We need to talk to Sandra about your pills."

Claire? Hmm. No, too neat and tidy. Wouldn't make sense, wouldn't be satisfying. Hannah? Hmm...

"Well... Hannah was shagging Stephen before Larry pancaked him. But I'm sure she was having an affair with Harvey?"

"Paul."

"Yes, love?"

"Harvey is a harvester. Farm equipment. Machinery, Paul."

"Right, right. I know that. So we're agreeing then? It's definitely Jurgita?"

Mary sighed, giving a fleeting stare to the bottle of red on the counter. Looked back at me and smiled deep.

"Well, maybe we go on a little date to the Paw tonight, Paul. We might be surprised by who we see there."

"Grand idea. I'll get my hi-vis. Safety first!"

I did have some concerns, though, and the professional thing to do would be to voice them.

"Mary? If they're running this drug enterprise, why would they publicly meet at the Paw?"

"That's... actually a good point, Paul."

She could have sounded a little less surprised by that. Wasn't I the cucumber ninja?

166

"Perhaps they're hiding in plain sight then, Paul? Or maybe it's a team-building exercise? Do drug dealers do that sort of thing?"

Of course! Mary's a bloody genius!

"I got it!" I blurted out. "Pizza parties for the dealers, love. And what do pizza parties need? Snacks! Bloody Jurgita."

Mary rolled her eyes. "Right then, Paul. Let's go over what we know, eat that leftover pizza, then head over."

The pizza seemed like a bad idea. It was important somehow, I was sure. But it was also dinner and we had to eat. Cruel fate, but the pizza wouldn't survive until sunrise.

Sat across from Mary most of the day, going over what we know. Even drew a doodle of what Gary, Harvey and Larry looked like, just to be extra helpful. It was soon approaching the early evening and we'd need to stake out the Bear's Paw.

"Paul, you don't bloody need to wear that," Mary groaned, tugging at my hi-vis jacket.

"Safety first, Mary."

She didn't reply, just wandered off to the car. Really should buy her one of these, help keep her safe—especially if we're taking on corner shop owners. They're tough gits.

Drive to the Paw didn't take long. Never really did, Wisbech under five minutes from Leverington. Still, can't help but wonder what we hoped to achieve by this. Give them a chance to explain themselves, maybe? Hear their side of the story?

Might have made more sense to take what we know to Tom. Bloody detective. Maybe take another crack at Harvey, get him to confess.

Still, we sat in our car, across the street. Made sure to wear all black to cancel out my hi-vis jacket. Cool like a cucumber, smart like a ninja.

"Just seen her go inside. Wait here, Paul," Mary said as she hopped out the car.

Damn, I was busy thinking about cucumbers and pancakes, and missed Jurgita. Why didn't Mary want me to follow? Was she in on this?

That wasn't a professional thought. Couldn't imagine Mary dealing dope to teenagers. Not her thing, that. She'd rather deal them life advice and a packet of crisps, which we still had dozens of back home.

Hold on a moment—there she bloody is! I'd recognise her anywhere, short little kingpin. Bloody Jurgita was round back with a van! Bet those bloody crisp boxes are in the back, too, probably full of something. Crisps, maybe? Or time.

Right then. Knees be damned as I hop out the car, head on over.

"Oh hi, Mr Paul!" she happily beamed as I stood next to her van. Right then, Mrs Kingpin, let's get down to business. Nice and cool like a penguin surfing.

"Jurgita, lovely to see you. So how do you feel about cannabis then?"

That should get her talking. Nice and subtle like the sunrise.

"Uh, excuse me? I think I not understand. Surely you don't mean drugs, Mr Paul?"

Hah! Going to play all innocent like a toddler dropping her ice cream cone, is she. Fine, we'll play along—for now.

I needed a plan—one as cunning as it was cheesecake. The drugs were in that van, and I needed a way to get her to admit that to me. Just had to think—this would need to be my smartest plan yet, given how bloody short she was.

"What you got in the back of that van then?" I asked carefully.

"Oh, take a look. I deliver nuts and crisps."

There they were. The snacks, just like I expected. It was all coming together—but where was the pizza? It was...

absent. Loud in its lack of presence. Was Jurgita just a cog in the machine? A small-time snack dealer caught up in a conspiracy?

"Mr Paul?"

"Sorry, love, sorry. I'll leave you to it, then. Best get to Mary. See you soon."

Smiled at each other as she walked the boxes round the back. Wonder what flavour crisps she had anyway? Hopefully not those bloody prawn cocktail. She could have mine back for all I cared. Bloody crisps.

Needed to get to Mary quick. She could be in danger, and she wasn't wearing a hi-vis jacket. Inside the Paw, stench of stale beer and lingering hints of tobacco. Dim lights and the dull droning chatter of pub patrons.

Ah, there we are—little corner table, Mary sat with Mark. Can't see the other two, obscured from here. Best shuffle over.

"Hey, Paul," Mark mumbled, arms folded like a pancake, beer in front of him.

He was sat with Mary, Jake and Hannah. Mood in here was tense—real tense. What was going—wait.

They had crisps. Crisps, nuts, and... pizza.

Pizza.

Pizza and pancakes.

Pizza and a criminal organisation run by... by...

"Lovely to see you, Paul," Hannah said, warm smile on her face. "Now sit."

Didn't really feel like a request, though said with the same gentle warmth she always displayed at improv. Felt more like a command wrapped in pastry. Yanked the chair out and plonked my knackered old knees down next to Mary.

Mark wouldn't meet my eyes. Just staring into his pint like it held the secrets of the stars.

Jake sat beside him, leaned back, same smug expression on his ugly mug with his arms folded like a pancake. Bloody stoner.

"You need to stop what you're doing, Hannah," Mary stated, steady as a Freddo. "You're profiting from kids, and—"

"Oh Mary," Hannah cut her off like a kingpin through a housewife, "I think you must be confused. What is it you think you know here?"

"I know about Harvey!" I blurted out.

Mary sat her hand on mine. "Settle down, Paul. We know about the cannabis, the distribution network, all of it."

Hannah took a sip from her wine. I thought I was cool as a cucumber, but her? Cool as a penguin sat on a glacier made of ice.

"I'm sure you're confused, Mary," Hannah calmly stated. "As far as I understand it, you only have one little video of a security guard and a small bag of weed. Mark assures me he's already been let go—isn't that right, Mark?"

Ah! Got them. That right there was a lie, spilling like a secret from Mark's cowering pancake. He can nod all he wants—that was a bunch of bull ox.

"He's lying," I responded. "Brian quit! I saw the whole thing. He didn't fire him. Stop being a bloody coward and tell the truth, Mark, it's unprofessional."

Jake started laughing, arms still folded and sat sentinel like a gargoyle statue. Had I said something funny? Or perhaps he was in on it with Harvey? Did Jake have Dick's blood on his hands?

"Right, thanks for that, Paul," Hannah said, kinda sending condescending tones my way. "Point is that was your one hook. You've nothing else."

"Call logs on Stephen's phone?" Mary sternly stated, staring at Hannah.

"So you're admitting to stealing property from a dead man? Gosh, you should go to the station and turn yourself in, Mary. That's illegal."

The iron wasn't lost on me. It sat in the kitchen, next to the board by the wall. But still a bit hypocritical considering she was a drug-dealing kingpin. Not the kind Hannah I'd come to know. Unprofessional, that.

"Well, what about those pizza deliveries with the bags of weed?" Mary pushed.

"Have you ever actually seen them, Mary?" Hannah responded gently. "All you have to go on is the word of your husband here, sat there in his hi-vis jacket in the middle of a pub, interviewing harvesters and talking to cheesecakes."

How the bloody hell did she know about Gary and Harvey? Well, I guess Harvey was obvious. She was sleeping with the star witness after all. Poor bloody Stephen pancake. Had I told her about Gary? Did I mention it out loud to someone? Bloody hell, I'm missing their little chat.

"Just chemicals, that's all. Nothing suspicious about the containers whatsoever."

"Wait!" I interjected. "Darren told me I know what's in them. I know that's where you're hiding the bloody cheesecakes."

Hannah reached across the table, gently set her hand on mine. Warm and kind, thoughtful, genuine.

"Paul, darling," she began. "You've been through a lot. Focus on your recovery, on your healing, on dealing with your trauma. You've witnessed two accidental deaths now. You need to do the work and—"

"Pizzas and pancakes," I cut her off quickly, her words choking me. Far too bloody unprofessional, that.

"You two go home, focus on each other. I'll see you at improv Friday, Paul. It'll be fun, I'm sure."

"You're up to no good, Hannah. We can talk to the police. We can—"

"Talk about what, Mary?" Hannah said, cutting her off like a sickle through wheat. "A conspiracy based on call logs from a stolen phone and pizza deliveries? You're a part-time cleaner. Paul a security guard with serious mental health issues. I sell farm machinery. None of us are exactly criminal masterminds now, are we?"

But she slipped up. Beautiful—admitted plain as day that she sold Harvey to the farm. I'm sure we can add that to the case.

"Bloody star witness," I muttered, grin on my face.

Hannah giggled. "There's my playful Paul. Go get some rest, and bring that energy to improv on Friday."

She stood to leave, Jake following suit. Bloody stoner.

"Drive safe. Be seeing you soon, Paul."

They walked out, Mary clenching her fists tight as they did. Mark still staring into his pint, like it held a key or a secret or a cheesecake that could crack this whole thing wide open. Sadly, it was just beer.

"Sorry," Mark simply said, ditching his pint, waltzing out after Hannah and the bloody stoner. Sodding coward.

Just like that Mary and I were alone at the table, surrounded by the droning of pub patrons and the stench of beer and victory. Not sure that could have gone any better, even if Jurgita was still at large.

"You alright, Paul?" Mary mumbled gently.

I honestly didn't know how to answer that. I was questioning everything—was I just an old man chasing pizzas and pancakes? Ghosts and conspiracies that didn't exist? I wanted to question the star witness, but it wouldn't help. He wouldn't talk anyway—he was just a bloody harvester.

"Great, Mary. Just great."

Lied through my teeth, and she knew it. Her smile was warm but wounded like a limping lion. Wish Gary the cheesecake would float down from the sky right now and just make everything all better like he did before. But he wasn't real, I had to see that. Maybe none of this was.

Guess it was time to leave. Couldn't sit here staring at Mark's pint forever—it wasn't talking either. Yeah, time to go home. Bloody pizzas and pancakes.

Chapter 27 - Not Hungry

Slept like a restless log last night. The ghosts don't bother me so much anymore, but from time to time I'd get a flashback or two. Watching Harvey laugh as he crushed Dick, but somehow Dick smiled, thumb raised. Was he happy to be at peace?

Or Larry, cackling maniacally as he distributed Stephen's biomechatronics across the road. Or was it biometrics? Biomelons? I'll have to ask Mary, I don't really get this science stuff.

Still, couldn't help but feel pretty victorious after our confrontation at the pub yesterday. I feel bad for Stephen, I know he loved Hannah. Tragic pancake, bloody Larry.

Mary doesn't seem herself. All morning, been sat in front of the telly, wine beside her. Not even watching anything, just staring into space. Was it a new channel? One that I couldn't see or hear? Didn't seem very professional, but how would I know?

Could ask her, but get the feeling she wants to be alone. Never seen her stare so hard at a bottle of wine before. Not sure she's even drunk any of it, come to think of it?

Well, seems I have a choice, doesn't it. Leave her be, head upstairs, go read Moby Dick. Yeah, think that seems like what I should do.

Yet found myself approaching her all the same. What was I bloody up to now?

"Mary, love," I started. "It'll be alright. Jurgita is only going to supply the pub with crisps and nuts from now on. No more pizzas and pancakes."

Mary looked happy, her smile curling down towards her chin. Eyes seemed dull, fight gone out of them. Definitely happy. Think this called for a celebration—I had just the plan.

"Mary, love? I know it's not really your thing, but why don't you come to improv tomorrow. Gang's all there— Hannah, the short guy with the moustache, that lady with the braces, short Simon, tall Simon, fictional Simon, Tom the detective—"

"Wait." Mary cut me off like a simile cutting into a metaphor. "That's right—that's right! Tom. He's a professional, right? You're always saying so."

Mary sprung up out of her chair, wine back in the fridge.

"Let's go to the police station, Paul. Look, we don't have much, I'll admit—and maybe we are chasing ghosts, but—"

"Pancakes," I incorrected.

"Sure, whatever. But we have to try, don't we, Paul? Let's go to our study, see what we can piece together. Could we maybe—"

Bloody professional, wife of mine. Spouting ideas like a kettle spouts steam. Wonder how you even make cheesecake anyway? Ah bloody hell, I'm not paying attention again.

"Do you think that'll work, Paul?"

There comes a time in every marriage where a husband has to admit the truth. Has to say sorry, love, wasn't listening, need you to repeat yourself please. Let's give it a shot.

"Yes dear, heard every word. Genius."

Bugger. I tried, I really did.

"Well come on then, Paul. Grab your hi-vis jacket, we're off to the police station."

Just like that, we were in the motor, on the way to the police station in Wisbech. Old courthouse, sat by the docks, truly a magnificent building to behold.

Not really sure how it works though. Do we have to make an appointment, or just wander in? Still, cunning cucumber ninja I was, I did come prepared.

"Here, love," I said, presenting Mary with a surprise as we pulled up in the nearby car park. "Put this on so we can remain anonymous."

Wore these disguises a lot at work, during those long winter nights. Soft fabric, covered your face, nice and simple.

"Paul," Mary said gently, "I'm not entering a police station wearing a bloody balaclava!"

Well, I tried. Guess we'd have to go in without them. She almost seemed upset with me.

"Just trying to help, love."

"I know, and I love you for that. Talk to Sandra about your pills tomorrow?"

"Will do. Think they're still there, actually—I asked them to follow me to the car, but they ignored me. Bloody ignorant pills."

Mary narrowed her gaze. "Uh... right. Well, let's go talk to Tom. That's his car, right?"

"Think it's the one with the reflective stripes, love. That's why I'm wearing my hi-vis, see—camouflage."

Police station stank of crime. Never expected crime to smell like floor polish and cheap coffee, but here we are.

"Hello, can we speak with Tom please?" Mary said to the desk lady doing her desk things from behind the logical glass.

Glass seemed to be divided into little square sections—make it easier to share, maybe?

"DCI Smith? He's a very busy man, you'll have to make an app—"

"No I won't," I blurted out. "I know him. He's my friend from improv. Let me see him. We're working on a very important pancake together."

"Sorry, but he's out at lunch right now, and you need an appointment. You can't just—"

"But he needs to interview the star witness!" I called out.

"Settle down, Paul," Mary said, gently stroking my arm. This didn't feel very professional—why couldn't I talk to my own friend? Tom and I cooked dragon egg omelettes together. That had to mean something.

Wait, or was that Stephen? No, no. I played chef with Hannah. Hannah! She was sleeping with them both. Wait—could she have been sleeping with Tom too?

Think, Paul. Did it make sense? It had to. Hannah liked to sleep, and so did Tom. So they definitely slept together—but—

"Paul? What are you doing here?" Tom asked, appearing from the nearby front door.

"Sorry, Tom, I told them you were out to lunch, but—"

"Don't worry, Julie, I'll handle it, thanks. Come on through."

Tom led us to a room. It wasn't a particularly nice one—it was bright, but not in a Gary the cheesecake way, more like a glaring into the back of your eyes kind of way. The room wanted my questions, and I had the answers. I could already feel myself cracking under the pressure like an omelette made of eggs.

"What's going on, Paul? Why are you here?"

Bloody hell. Sat across the bright white table from Tom, I felt exposed. Thank god I was in camouflage. Really should have worn that balaclava, though.

"Pizzas and pancakes," I replied, staring Tom right in the eyes. That should answer both his questions in a neat little bow.

"Right, I've just had lunch. Not hungry. Well, this has been fascinating, but I've got work to do, criminals to catch."

Tom stood, gesturing to the door.

"Sit," Mary commanded. He looked surprised, the kind of look a man gave when he was used to taking orders only from his boss.

Tom obliged, grin on his face. "Mary, wasn't it? Haven't seen you in... forever, really. Gave up on improv?"

"Didn't like Hannah. Could never quite place why— maybe deep down I always knew she was a drug-dealing guard-crushing kingpin?"

Tom's smile escaped. Not sure where it fled to, but it certainly wasn't on his face anymore. Couldn't say the same about his moustache, though, still littered his face like a messy playground.

"I'm not sure what you think you know, but you're mistaken. Leave it alone."

"Are you actively investigating her?"

"Nothing to investigate. Drop it, go home, order a pizza or something. We're done here." Tom stood once more.

"I have video evidence," Mary stated.

"Show me," Tom said, sitting back down.

Mary pulled out her phone, showing Tom a brief video of Brian and the bag of weed. Tom twiddled his moustache, but I couldn't understand why. Was it important somehow? I was missing something, I was sure of it.

"So, just do as I've said, alright?"

"Can do," Mary said, sullen look on her face. I missed what Tom said. There comes a time in every marriage, where a husband has to—

"Heard every word, mate," I blurted out. "Genius. So when do we arrest her?"

"We don't, Paul. Just a bag of weed and I don't see Hannah in that video, do you? Just go home, and stop wasting police time."

Tom stood, chair scraping across the floor as he did, gesturing for us to exit.

Drive home was silent. But not the kind of comfortable silence that a man and wife share across the study table, the kind of silence when you find a Dick pancake crushed by Harvey the harvester.

Mary didn't say a word. Straight to the fridge, happily humming away, wine to her table. Poured herself a glass and stared at the telly, on the secret channel once more. I couldn't hear or see a thing.

It would be OK. I wasn't going to let Mary down, or anyone down. Tomorrow was Friday—improv day. And I was going to get Harvey, the star witness, his day in court. Paul Hope is on the case, and I had never once known defeat. Victory would be mine.

"Paul, come sit," Mary mumbled solemnly.

"What's up, love? Didn't that go well?"

"No. It didn't. He dismissed us, doesn't care about the evidence. Just a bag of weed, he said. She's won, and she's laughing at us."

Poor Mary. Couldn't see the victory right in front of her, lost in the pizzas the pancakes and the cheesecakes. All we had to do was show up at improv, and the rest would fall into place. I had a plan, and like a cucumber ninja with a bone, I wasn't letting it go.

"You'll see, Mary. We don't need Tom. We just need each other," I mumbled, but she didn't hear me. The call of her wine screamed over me, and I just couldn't get a bloody word in edgeways.

Chapter 28 - The Day I Pancake

"So how have you been, Paul?"

Found myself back in Sandra's office. Had to wait a bloody long while, they seem behind today. Maybe everyone else was dealing with their own pizzas and pancakes? Who knew. Still, my bloody pills should follow me this time—if they don't, I might—

"Paul?"

"Sorry, sorry. Off with the pancakes."

"Ah. Thinking about your dead colleagues?"

"Try not to. But I cracked the case now—Jurgita has promised she'll only deal crisps and nuts from now on. No more cheesecakes."

Tapping away at her keyboard as I spoke. Probably writing me a letter of commendation again, finally getting me the attention of His Majesty. About bloody time.

"Paul, I noted you didn't collect your pills last time. Are you unmedicated?"

"Of course not!" I interjected. "Graduated with my O-levels years ago."

Bloody unprofessional, that. Have her know I'm the smartest person I don't know. Bloody therapists.

"Right, well, if your wife is with you, maybe she can help you collect them?"

"Bloody good idea," I agreed. "Little bastards ignored me last time. Sodding pills, think they're better than me."

"I see."

Tapping away on her bloody keyboard again. Tappity tap tap. How many bloody commendations do I need, Sandra? Honestly, she must be impressed.

"You'll be seeing me more often, Paul, if that's alright. And I've upped your dosage a little—please, make sure you take your pills."

"If the little buggers cooperate, sure!"

Obviously never found herself arguing with a pill before. Surprises me really, given that she's a doctor. Knows more about pancakes than I do, that's for sure.

"So tell me more about this little investigation of yours then, Paul. What have you found out?"

Hold on a bloody minute. That was professional. Too professional.

Jesus Christ.

Was Sandra the—no. No, couldn't be. It was Jurgita. Probably.

"We met at the pub. All my friends were there—Mark, Jake, Hannah. All but Gary the cheesecake. Oh, and the pancakes, obviously."

"Of course."

Tippity-tappity-type. More bloody letters of commendation. Seriously, Sandra, I'm professional enough already.

"Hannah seems to be running the thing, probably orders from Jurgita."

"Does that make sense, Paul? A corner shop owner running a criminal empire, or a woman with connections, access to farms, distribution networks? Have a think."

A think? Bloody hell, how much would that cost? Fine, fine. Time to sit and think.

Hannah. Farm equipment sales. Harvey the star witness came from her company. She sold it to the farm where he pancaked Dick. Did he do it on her orders, or was it a crime of passion?

Hannah and the love triangle. Sleeping with Stephen and Harvey at the same time. That's why he killed himself—it was no bloody accident. He was heartbroken. Larry was no murderer, just an innocent lorry, ran into Stephen at the wrong place, wrong time. Stephen must have known you can't hug a lorry and live.

Hannah. At the pub. With Mark, who owns the pizza place and the Paw itself. He said he was owned, didn't he? By Jake, or by Hannah? Or does Hannah own Jake who owns Mark? This was getting complicated.

"Bugger," I muttered.

"What is it, Paul?"

"Hannah framed Jurgita. She's the bloody kingpin, isn't she?"

"Paul, you're unmedicated and deeply disturbed. If you have these concerns, you should be careful to avoid the people involved, and if you have evidence you should approach the police."

Bloody hell, why does she keep calling me uneducated? Told her about my—wait.

Unmedicated? She means my bloody pills! Sodding things haven't been helping me because I haven't been taking them. And I haven't been taking them because they didn't follow me home!

I could be imagining this whole bloody conspiracy.

But no. I wasn't. Hannah made sense. But why was she so kind, so gentle, so dismissive?

Mary was right. Harvey and Hannah planned this whole bloody thing together. They deal drugs to kids and Dick got caught in their crossfire. They had to kill him—he could tell Stephen Hannah was cheating when he joined improv.

So... they killed him because I invited him to improv, and Dick knew about Hannah and Harvey.

Dick died because of me.

Fuck.

"I... I killed Dick, didn't I?" I muttered to Sandra, tears fleeing my eyes. Little buggers, bloody unprofessional.

"No, Paul. Talk this out with me."

Sat and talked with Sandra for another ten minutes. I was stuck in a maze, a labyrinth, every road led me to myself, always pointing and laughing at Dick pancake chewed up by Harvey's mouth.

But I was wrong. I'm no villain. I'm a doddering old git of a security guard.

Before long, the pieces began to click like a puzzle made of cheesecakes. Hannah did all of this. It's all her fault. Jurgita was caught in her crossfire, just like Dick, just like Stephen.

The wool was pulled into my eyes this whole time. No wonder they hurt, rubbing them as the tears dried up. Must have run out—not cheap, those.

"From everything we've discussed, Paul, she sounds dangerous, and I think you should talk seriously with the police. You need to make sure you take your medicine, and soon."

"I'm exposing her tonight at improv. That detective, Tom, is there. He's working with us now, I'm sure. Though he did tell us to bugger off at the station."

Bugger, he did, didn't he? Does Hannah own him too? Does she own—does she own me?

No. Marriage contract, Paul. I am Mary's, and will be till the day I pancake.

"I don't think you should go, Paul. You need to recover, heal, take your pills, attend thera—"

Bloody hell she was boring. Running her mouth like a fridge. Or a runner? They run too. No idea. Oh, I'm missing something again.

"So can you commit to that please, Paul? For your own good?"

"Heard every word," I said truthfully. "I'll go do that."

"Good. See you Monday, Paul."

Right then. I didn't need the star witness, because the star witness was me. I'm taking you down, Hannah Rogers and Harvey Harvesterson. This little drug operation of yours is coming to an end, then I'm popping home to Mary to eat a celebratory Gary.

I gestured for the prescription to follow me, but it didn't. Bloody thing. Guess I'll have to carry it like a bloody baby. Honestly, pills could be so unprofessional.

Well then. It was off to improv, and tonight, it would be extra special. Agent Paul Hope, reporting for duty.

Chapter 29 - Zip Zap Pancake

"I'm off to improv, love. You coming with?"

Didn't say anything. Sat in her armchair, wine beside her, soaps on the bloody telly once more. Guess she wasn't feeling very professional right now.

Well don't you worry, Mary. Agent Paul Hope is on the case, and I'm taking them all down. I've got a plan for improv tonight, and like the rest of my plans so far? It's bound to go swimmingly.

Grip the wheel extra tight as I pull into the car park of the community centre. I can already smell the cheap floor polish and even cheaper coffee.

Stephen's car was still here. Guess that makes him first tonight, though I don't imagine he'll be with us, pancake and all. They just keep slapping on more tickets, but Stephen couldn't pay them even if he wanted to.

Hannah was here too. Car sat out front, same spot as always. Brought my hi-vis jacket, make sure I'm safe—couldn't let Mary or the pancakes or anyone down. Tonight was the night, and I came prepared.

Knees didn't protest on my approach to the community centre tonight. For once they seemed to agree with me. Felt good to finally be in sync with myself.

Could see Hannah setting up chairs same as ever. Nice circle, couple of Simons helping out. Fictional Simon didn't, though. Lazy bastard couldn't even be bothered to exist.

Right then. Hannah smiled at me, same warm, professional smile she wore like a mask, hiding her rotten apple beneath. I could finally see her, and at last, it was showtime. Took a deep breath, then at long last,

"Hi, Hannah! Lovely to see you," I said. If that didn't get her sweating, I don't know what would.

"Paul, dear, glad you're here. How's everything?"

Knew that would get her sweating. Could see her about to crack like a duck egg. Why specifically a duck? No idea, but eggs were eggs.

Guess chocolate eggs weren't eggs, though. They didn't have goo in them. Apart from those Creme Eggs. Or caramel ones. Or—

"Paul?"

"Bloody hell, sorry, Hannah. Off with the chocolate eggs. So how's Harvey then?"

That should apply some gentle pressure. Knew full well they were shagging, and the casual mention would throw her off guard.

"Oh dear, Paul. Are you sure you're alright to be here? You seem confused. First you think I'm dating a harvester, next you think I'm a kingpin! Hilarious."

Something about her words felt very professional. A little too much so, in fact. Still, I hadn't played all my cards yet—more regulars arrived, including Stephen and Tom.

Not Stephen, Darren. Stephen's a pancake. Keep it together, Paul.

More zips, zaps and pancakes and we were ready to get going.

Hannah and Darren stood ready to play. Darren looked particularly professional tonight—smile curling downwards, sweat on his brow, eyes darting around the room like hungry flies.

"Well, we need a prompt. Paul, you're feeling particularly creative tonight—mind coming up with one?"

Bloody hell. Just like that, I was on the spot. Plan was not going to plan, which I didn't plan for. Should have planned for that. Bugger.

"I've got one for you," I said, nice and calm, nice and professional. "You're an evil bitch dealer who sells drugs to kids, and Darren's a trapped accomplice."

Nice and simple one to start. Should be easy to act out, they already know their parts like the back of their hands.

Hannah's scowl could just about set my face on fire if she stared any harder. But we were both distracted by Tom, sat cackling like a bloody hyena.

"Christ, Paul. You're gonna bloody love this."

Tom rose from his seat, stepped into the middle and slapped a pair of cuffs on Hannah like a detective catching a crook.

"Hannah Rogers, you're under arrest for the conspiracy to commit blackmail, supply and distribute class C illegal substances. You have the right—"

Bloody boring, not even Tom's turn. Bloody hell was he playing at? Hold on, I should probably pay attention to this. Some bloody good acting.

"You can't do this!" Hannah shrieked like a banshee.

"It's already done. Let's go down the station for a proper chat, shall we?"

"Wait!" The word burst out before I could stop it, Tom already carting Hannah off like a shopping trolley. Couldn't help myself, had to know: "Why'd you flatten Dick like a pancake? Why not just leave Stephen for Harvey?"

Hannah scowled at me. "Paul, you doddering old nincompoop, I deal weed, Harvey is farm equipment, and I'm not a bloody killer."

Wait... what?

"So it was a... a bloody accident?"

"Yes, you bloody twit!" she yells, Tom ferrying her away.

"Bloody hell. Was I just chasing pancakes and pizzas this whole time?" I say to nobody in particular.

"No, mate," Darren chimes in. "You were instrumental. Without you—"

"Instrumental? I ain't a bloody saxophone, am I, mate?" I sang like a church choir.

Darren laughed out loud. "No, mate. But you got me to sing from your hymn sheet. Thought about what kind of father I want to be, just like you said, and... this kind, mate. The kind that stands up for what's right."

I had to admit, I was bloody confused—he was already standing, it was his turn to act. I'm fairly sure my plan worked like a charm, though—Hannah arrested, Tom my man on the inside like I always knew he would be. Bloody professional, me.

Wonder when military intelligence would try to recruit me. All those commendations from Sandra, I was a shoe-in. Or was it a trainer? Can't remember.

"Wait a minute," I mutter. "Without bloody Hannah, who will run improv?"

Darren put his hand on my shoulder, firm and friendly. "Can't think of anyone better than you, mate. Lead the way."

Me? Well, I was a secret agent, a cucumber ninja and Gary's best mate. Why the bloody hell not?

"After going through all that, feel like improv should become group therapy club," fictional Simon didn't say.

Not a bloody bad idea that, to be fair. If I'm honest with myself, this was pretty much therapy for me anyway. Right then, think that was enough drama for tonight—off to go home, see the wife, have some dinner.

Chapter 30 - Extra Cheese

Rest of improv didn't quite have the same mood to it as usual. Probably because everyone went home early—Tom and Hannah really did commit to the bit. Best bloody actors I've ever seen, so professional.

Tapped my fingers happily on the steering wheel as I drove home. Something about tonight felt good, but couldn't place my finger on why. Dick pancake behind my eyes but not angry, like before. Just seemed calm now, like he was at peace.

Shame that Harvey was still at large, though. Bloody harvester wouldn't have his day in court after all. Least they got Hannah, and that was a start I s'pose.

Pulled into my driveway, pushed through my front door. Mary still in her armchair, bottle half empty. Not bad, thought she might be on her second by now.

"Hi, love," I say, sitting down nearby. "How was your evening?"

"Fine, Paul. Just fine."

She said the words, but the professionalism was gone. Too bad she didn't come to improv—was a bloody good session, she would have enjoyed it.

"That reminds me," I say, "I'm the troop leader at improv now."

Mary looked at me, sunken eyes, smile curling down. Almost looked right through me like I was fictional Simon.

"What? Why? Hannah and her twisted sense of humour no doubt?"

"Hannah is a bloody good actor, love."

"Yeah. I'll say. Too bad she'll never pay for her crimes."

Mary took another sip of her wine, it laughing at me as she did. Bloody wine, always trying to come between me and my wife.

"You missed a really good show tonight, dear. Tom acted for once. Carted Hannah off in handcuffs."

Mary's eyes opened closed, mouth agape ready for a Gary. Bugger, did I leave him in the car? Or forget to buy him completely? I forgot. I was hungry, that I couldn't doubt. All these bloody pizzas and pancakes.

"Paul? You're serious?"

Studying my face like there was an exam. Bloody hell, I didn't do any revision at all. No way I'm passing this one.

"Yes, love, got a photo and everything. Felt so bad about not getting a photo of that pizza weed I got one of this."

Showed her the photo, she stared at it like it just called her a bloody cow.

"Anyway, I'm hungry, love. You had your tea yet? I'm thinking pizza?"

"What the bloody hell! Paul! Paul! You—you bloody did it! Paul!"

Mary erupted like a bottle of champagne, spilling her wine on the thirsty carpet. Bloody hell, I wasn't about to fund two drinking habits.

Leapt out her chair, arms around me, hugging me warm and tight. Bit unprofessional, but I wasn't about to complain—though my sodding stomach might, gargling away like a gargoyle.

"This is bloody real, Paul! You did it!"

"Yeah, told you. Tom's very professional. And me, well, not bad for a cucumber ninja cat at all, is it?"

"You are AMAZING, Paul Hope! I love you so much!"

Bloody hell. Not sure what I did, but she seemed real happy. Smile was upside down now, eyes full of that same glint I saw in Gary's, when that glorious cheesecake bastard swung by for a visit to gift me a rubber ruler.

"How the bloody hell did you do this, Paul?"

"What? Oh, that was simple. Wore my trusty hi-vis jacket—works every time."

"Christ, Paul, wear that thing the next time you buy a lottery ticket, won't you?"

Bugger! Why had I never thought of that? Wife's a bloody genius.

Tears were streaming down her face now, betraying her upturned frown. Had I upset her? Probably.

"Should have thought of that sooner, sorry, love. I can tell you're hungry, since you're crying and all. Pizza?"

"Just overjoyed, you old nitwit. Love you, Paul. Pizza sounds great, but Paul?"

"No, love?"

"Not from that bloody Spicy Pizza Palace place, please!"

Couldn't help myself, started chuckling like a juggler. Mary followed right along. Ocean felt like a stream tonight. Very professional.

Seems I had my next mission, then. Phone in my hand, hi-vis jacket round my shoulders, Agent Paul Hope reporting for duty.

Tapped the buttons carefully. Had to get this right. Not a bloody travesty like last time.

"Pizza Penguin, order please?"

Young man on the phone sounded very professional—I'd have to be bloody careful. Focus, Paul.

"Do the pizzas come with free penguins?"

"Sir, no. Now what do you want please?"

"Pizza."

"Right, I gathered that. But what kind?"

Bugger. I knew I should have studied—this exam was hard. But I needed that grade, and I was going to pass.

"Cucumber."

"Sir, we don't do—"

"Pancake."

"We don't bloody sell—"

"Cheese!"

"Right, bloody finally, thank you. Forget to take your pills, old man?"

"Yeah. Bloody things didn't follow me home again. Bastards."

"Uh... right. Well what size?"

Here we bloody go again. Focus, damn it, Paul. And why is Mary giggling so hard? Was I not nailing this? Felt professional. Probably.

"Cheese please."

"Yes, size?"

"Cheese."

"CHRIST! They don't pay me enough for this bullshit! Sir, what bloody size of pizza do you—"

"Extra cheese!"

"SIR! Extra cheese isn't a bloody size! What size do you want for fuc—"

"Extra!"

"GREAT! Bloody extra-large pizza with bloody extra cheese. I don't care if you want anything else, you're not getting it. Delivery in half an hour, twenty quid cash. Bye."

Ah. Hung up on me. Not very professional, that. Mary seemed to be having fun, though—haven't seen her laugh like that in a while.

"I love you so bloody much, Paul."

"Love you too, Mary. Pizza time. Can't wait."

"Me either. We'll share it with a film, Paul, and you can regale me with a tale about cheesecakes and pancakes and bloody everything, Paul."

"Might take a while, love. There's Gary, Harvey, Larry—"

"We've all night, Paul."

Pizza came soon after that. Bloody huge box again—were these things getting bigger? Still, plenty left for breakfast.

Wine bottle stayed in the fridge. Mary didn't seem to want it anymore. Didn't matter, pizza would keep it company for now. Pizzas and pancakes.

Chapter 31 - Heard every word

Here we go again. Phone in my hand, hand shaking. Time to do this again, one more mission, one more cucumber ninja.

Hannah behind bars. Probably. Improv mine? Guess so. But it was time for my most challenging mission yet, and I came prepared. Sat at the kitchen table, hi-vis jacket round my shoulders, and tapping in the numbers.

The phone rang. Time to be professional. I had to get this right, there was no room for error. I was connected, and the show was time.

"Hi mate, tea?" I casually said.

"Sure mate, be right round," Darren said, call ending with a click.

Bloody hell, that was close. But true to form, Paul the professional, the cucumber ninja, the ginger tabby cat dancing in the rain. Darren would soon be here, then it was time for my next challenging mission—make a cup of tea.

"That Darren, love?" Mary said. "I'll pop the kettle on then."

Bloody love this woman, a true professional, through and through. Picked up my slack, popping on the kettle, tea soon be ready.

Moments passed. Minutes, maybe? Definitely some seconds. Those were slippery bastards, in my experience.

Doorbell rang out like a bell ringing, announcing his approach. Mary pulled open the door, letting him inside.

"Hi Darren," she said softly, beckoning him to the kitchen table where my knees sat in preparation. "Good to see you."

"You too. Hi Paul. Figured I owed you guys a bit of an explanation? You know, about, well... everything."

"The pizzas and the pancakes?" I blurted.

"Yes mate. Exactly that."

Darren settled into his chair, taking his cup of tea. Two sugars, one milk, one tea, one cup. Why two sugars when one of everything else, I had to wonder? Something very ginger tabby cat about that.

Was good to see Darren looking more professional. No sweat on his brow, no stress on his lips, wearing jeans and a t-shirt. Bit of a contrast to the bloody arrest scene at improv last night. Mad, that.

"How's the baby?" Mary asked. I assume she meant his cat, but could have meant his wife's baby.

"She's doing well. Got her sorted. So yeah, Hannah arrested. Pretty wild, right?"

"I'll say," I said. "Jurgita still bloody at large though. Bloody Tom, such an amateur. Not very professional."

"Settle down, Paul. How the hell did you all pull this off then? I thought Paul was mad—well, he is a little, but clearly not!"

Darren chuckled, hand on my shoulder. "This bloody legend is as sane as you or me. Well, sort of. But if Paul hadn't asked me what kind of father I wanted to be? I might still be sat under Hannah's thumb."

"So Hannah was in charge, then? Did she kill Dick with that harvester?"

"Harvey," I corrected. "Star witness."

Mary squeezed my hand, putting me at ease. Bloody professional, this wife of mine. Hold on, missing Darren speaking various words, maybe even a sentence or two.

"So because of Paul, yeah. Went to Tom, and yeah, Hannah will get some time. Fair bit, I expect. Poor bloody Stephen."

Poor bloody Stephen indeed. Hannah, cheating on him with Harvey. So upset he decided to cuddle Larry the lorry, but he forgot Larry weighs more than ten tonnes. Pancaked him flat like a pancake.

"So there were others?" Mary asked, after various other questions. Bloody hell, missed those too. Should I tell them I'm not keeping up with all this? Probably should.

"Heard every word," I truthfully announced. "Bloody professional team effort."

"Absolutely mate, absolutely. Yeah, blackmail on Stephen, Mark, and others," Darren said, offering me a warm smile. Bloody hell, wish he was here earlier, could have fried my eggs on that.

So Hannah was emailing more than just Stephen and Harvey? Mark too? Bloody hell. Her inbox must be full. Unprofessional, that.

"So the harvester... really was a tragic accident," Mary muttered.

"Tragic pancake," I corrected. She sure wasn't on the ball at the moment—conversation must be more professional than I realised.

"Yeah, afraid so. And who knows what happened to Jake—vanished the night we moved on Hannah. Tom isn't concerned, though—got himself the win he wanted," Darren stated.

"No wonder he ushered us out of the police station, then. Couldn't let us interfere with your investigation."

Didn't I already bloody tell her that? Swear Mary had a listening problem. Still, loved her all the same anyway. Oh dear, Darren was talking again. Focus, Paul.

"Heard every word," I announced. "Pizzas and pancakes."

"What exactly was in the containers at the farm?" Mary asked.

"Pancakes. Full of them," I proudly stated. Fine night of infiltration, that. Interrogated Harvey like a proper cucumber ninja.

"If pancakes means cannabis, then yeah. Right bloody lot. But all sorted now," Darren corrected incorrectly. Didn't bloody know his pancakes from his cannabis at his age, silly sausage. Wait, how bloody old was he anyway?

"What puzzles me," Mary mumbled, "is how Hannah seemed so simple, normal, nice."

"Yeah," Darren replied. "Tom said that's how it goes, usually. Smartest criminals often kept their hands clean and wore two faces."

"She laughed about the star witness," I said suddenly, the memory hitting me like a lorry hitting Stephen. "At the farm. When I made that joke about Harvey being a murderer, she laughed so hard. Thought it was hilarious."

"That's because she knew it was just faulty equipment," Darren said gently. "She wasn't worried about being caught for that because there was nothing to catch her for. Dick's death was just tragic timing—made you suspicious, made you start digging, and that digging eventually led to us taking her down."

"So Dick died for nothing?" I asked, feeling that familiar mutiny in my knees.

"No, mate," Darren said firmly. "Dick died in an accident. But his death led to all this being exposed. Led to those kids not getting drugs anymore. Led to those blackmail victims being freed. Dick didn't die for nothing at all."

Mary squeezed my hand again. Ocean felt like a stream today. Maybe even a puddle.

"Well, all worked out in the end, then. Mostly," Mary mused, offering me a smile like a wounded doe.

"Yeah. But he'll be fine. Tough old git, aren't you Paul?" Darren stated, patting my shoulder again. Were he and my shoulder friends? They seemed to be.

"Too bloody right mate. All professional, all cucumber, me."

"All cucumber indeed, mate. Well, I'd best head back to work. After my bloody community service, of course."

Just like that, Darren was gone. Tea was drained and he was out the door. Mary and I together again, sipping our own teas.

"So what now?" Mary asked eventually.

"Fancy a proper Gary. Lemon one. To celebrate."

"Celebrate what?"

"Pizzas and pancakes. We solved the pizzas and pancakes."

Mary kissed my cheek. "Why not? Off to the corner shop, then. But no more bloody boxes of crisps!"

Finally felt like I wasn't chasing pancakes anymore for the first time in a while. The puzzle glued together nicely, all pieces firmly in place. Probably.

Things were gonna be alright, I was sure. More than alright—proper professional.

Epilogue

Back on patrol now. Same car, same routes, same uniform—different Paul and a different sodding logo. Securotech Solutions, whatever the bloody hell that means. Logo cost the boss a grand, but took his designer about a minute. Probably.

Nice guy, this Gary Stone fella. Not as delicious as Gary the sentient cheesecake, but still a professional. Think back to that dream often, smile on my face as I do.

Parked up in a lay-by, on my break. Gazing up at the stars, wondering what's up there. Aliens and cheesecakes, probably. Or probably not. Not finding out in my bloody lifetime, that's for sure.

Break doesn't last long—but at least I got hands-free.

"Hi, love," I say, chipper as a chipmunk with cheeks full of acorns. "How's your evening then?"

"Just wanted to wish you goodnight, I'm off to bed. Hope the rest of your shift is qu—goes well."

Couldn't help but chuckle at that. She remembered the Q-word, forbidden amongst security guards. Bloody love my Mary.

"Thanks, love, sweet dreams. I'll see you tomorrow—you coming to my improv club?"

"Wouldn't miss it, dear. Night night."

Lovely. Mary off to sleep, but I've another six hours on the road. Still, I wouldn't be lonely—Darren and Claire to see, sites to patrol, even a new guard or two to train as well.

Pull up to the storage facility, Darren at the guard hut waiting.

"Evening, mate," I say, approaching his window. "How's it going?"

"Yeah, all good, mate. You seem a lot better lately—happy for you, Paul."

Suppose I was, really. Was it the pills, the therapy, the passing of the time? Who could say. I knew I wasn't the same as I was before, though—something had snapped, and though the pieces were back together, they'd never quite be the same again.

"So what do you think, mate?"

Oh bugger. Wasn't bloody listening again, was I. That got annoying a while ago, but I just can't seem to snap out of it, even with the... lack of pancakes.

"Heard every word," I truthfully said. Probably.

"Paul, mate, knock it off. You're as good a liar as Hannah was a kingpin."

Couldn't help but chuckle at that. "Christ, Darren, bit bloody harsh that. Can't believe she was blackmailing Stephen. I thought all along they were bloody lovers."

Darren shook his head. "Don't want to speak ill of the pancakes, mate, as you say, but his ugly mug? Out of his league, her."

"Oh I don't know. Not got a patch on my Mary, mate. Besides, dealing to kids does kind of make her ugly inside and out."

"Bloody hell, Paul. Bit profound for you, ain't it, mate?"

Maybe it was. Didn't really mind—job like mine gave you a lot of time to think. Besides, I'd agreed to do static half the time now. Nice quiet nights were what I needed after all the bloody pizzas and pancakes.

"Got anything special planned for improv tomorrow night then, Paul?" Darren asked.

"Just you wait and see, mate. Finally got Claire to agree to join us. I'm sure it'll be a riot."

"Can't bloody wait, mate. Bit of a break from the wailing baby!"

"Well, I'm glad that all worked out, Darren. Still—must be off, got my rounds to do. Seeya later, mate."

Hopped back in the motor, stupid bloody logo taunting me as I did. The more things change, the more they stay the same, or something like that.

Scene: In my motor, off on mobile patrol. Prompt: bloody bored, but soon be home time.

Action.

Printed in Dunstable, United Kingdom